CLASSIC DUTCH-BUILT COASTERS

by

Bernard McCall

A product of Scheepswerf Appingedam v/h A. Apol, this coaster was launched as *Dicky* on 3 April 1958 and delivered on 26 June to Albertus Westera, of Appingedam. Management was in the hands of the Wagenborg company. She was fitted with a 6-cylinder Brons engine of 395bhp which was replaced in 1975 by a 6-cylinder Praha of 700bhp. The most notable feature of her career occurred in 1963 when she sailed from Spain to Hull, but via Montevideo and Punta Arenas (Argentina), Valparaiso and Iquique (Chile), Callao (Peru), and via the Panama Canal to Barranquilla (Colombia) before heading across the Atlantic. The voyage of 18,400 nautical miles was accomplished without problems. She became *Vera T* in mid-November 1974 after being sold to Rotterdam-based Vertom. Sold to Panamanian-flag operators two years later, she was renamed *Kiti* and the next decade saw a series of name changes as she became *Ebony* (1977), *Cris* (1978), *Rovalma* (1980), *Cris* again (1982), *Sea Lady* (1983) and finally *Cris* for a third time in 1985. On Christmas Day 1986 she sank when two miles off Bissau after leaving that port for Conakry with a cargo of fertiliser. Her crew was rescued by a trawler and put ashore in Dakar.

(Neil Burns)

INTRODUCTION

The term classic Dutch coasters requires some explanation. As far as this book is concerned, it covers mainly a twenty year period between 1950 and 1970. Most of the coastal ships built during this period had cargo handling gear and some were able to navigate tortuous narrow rivers in addition to undertaking worldwide voyages. All the ships featured in this book were built in the Netherlands although not all sailed under the Dutch flag, and all were built prior to 1970.

The Dutch coastal trades developed rapidly through the twentieth century following the introduction of motor coasters. Traditionally coasters had been owned by families with ships passing from one generation to the next along with the knowledge to operate and trade them successfully. A new generation of captain/owners started to appear. These were men who had left deepsea trades and then bought a coaster or they were former crewmen who wanted to own their own vessel. Although they were good sailors, they lacked the background, the contacts and the business acumen to trade their ships successfully. As a consequence, some captain/owners established their own trade associations in order to pool knowledge and optimise trading possibilities. There were several well-known chartering offices/cargo houses in the northern Netherlands that looked after the commercial management of coasters and also provided an excellent link to the many building yards in that part of the country. These included Carebeka, Gruno, Kamp's, Wagenborg, Wijnne & Barends along with Spliethoff in Amsterdam. Some of them were only managers and brokers but others also owned ships.

The heyday of the Dutch coaster was the early 1960s when over 1000 were in service. All had a gross tonnage of under 500grt. Above that figure, the ships had to be manned according to deep sea regulations and so they would no longer be economic to operate. Deciding on the order of presentation within the book was no easy matter. In the end I decided to arrange the photographs so that we begin with the oldest and end with the newest. There is a small group that will be exempted from that sequence as will be explained in the relevant captions.

As the 1960s progressed, competition increased in the coastal trades and the ships increased in size in order to carry more cargo. Dutch yards also began to build more coasters for owners outside the Netherlands. Some of these are included as they offer contrasting designs. With one exception, this book features coasters that did not appear in our two earlier books *Coasters of the 1950s* and *Coasters of the 1960s*.

Acknowledgements

I thank all the photographers who have made their work available for publication. Much information has been obtained from the Dutch website marhisdata.nl. I also thank my Dutch friends Ben Th. Gernaat, Koos Goudriaan, Bert Kruidhof and Ben Scholten who have checked the text. As always I thank Gil Mayes for his thorough checking of early drafts. My grateful thanks once again to the Amadeus Press for their fine printing.

Bernard McCall   Portishead   April 2015

Front cover : A well-travelled coaster, the **Biak** was built by Scheepswerf Appingedam v/h A. Apol and was driven by a 6-cylinder Brons engine of 395bhp. Launched on 24 October 1957, she was delivered to Groningen-based W H Roelfs on 6 February 1958. Initially managed by Gruno, she transferred to Carebeka management in 1965. The first of her peregrinations began at Cairnryan in Scotland later in 1958. She left on 26 August and sailed to Yokohama via Durban, Saigon and South Korea. She returned via Bandar Shahpour (Iran), the Suez Canal, Iskenderun, Piraeus, Cartagena and Bordeaux, eventually arriving in Rotterdam on 23 February 1959. On 25 November 1959 she grounded in the River Elbe when on passage from Västerås to Antwerp and refloated without problem two days later. She was on her travels again in 1960 and grounded on a sandbank in the River Paraná. A drydocking near Asunción two weeks later revealed no damage. In the late 1960s, she was chartered by the Netherlands Offshore Company for seismological work and was fitted with extra steelwork at the stern. A more serious grounding on a reef off Great Abacon Island in the Bahamas on 17 September 1992 caused serious damage and she was towed to Jacksonville for repairs. In November 1999 she was arrested in Miami for drugs smuggling. Changes of name saw her become **Biak I** in 1999, **Sabra X** in 2000 then revert to **Biak** in 2005. She was thought to have survived at least until 2013. We see her outward bound in the Manchester Ship Canal on 9 October 1977.

(C J Tabarin, courtesy Neil Burns)

Back cover : This coaster was built at the Martenshoek shipyard of Hijlkema & Zonen. She was launched on 4 January 1962 and delivered as **Ali** on 10 April to Haiko Havinga, of Groningen. Management was entrusted to Wijnne & Barends. She had a 5-cylinder Brons engine of 220bhp. In October 1974, she hoisted the Red Ensign after purchase by Carisbrooke Shipping, based at Cowes on the Isle of Wight. She was renamed **Helena-C**. She remained in this company's ownership for eight years. In 1982 she was sold to operators in the Caribbean for trading under the flag of the Cayman Islands. For most of her career with Carisbrooke, her two masts and two 2-tonne derricks were removed but they were replaced after her sale. She left Sluiskil on 26 October 1982 with Paramaribo as her destination. She proved to be a handy vessel for trading in the West Indies with occasional voyages to the USA. On 18 May 1983, for example, she left Port Castries for Guyana but on 8 July she left Philadelphia for Port Canaveral. At this time, it was reported that she was to be renamed **Alro Trader** but this never happened. After arrival at Miami in March 1985, she was arrested for smuggling. She is next reported in early 1990 when she was sold and renamed **Melinda D**. This was very shortlived. On 14 April 1990 she sank on the edge of the Great Bahama Bank, some 180 miles south-east of Miami, when carrying a cargo of vehicles. We see her about to pass under the Humber Bridge on 23 September 1981.

(David Gallichan)

It would require a page or more to write a full history of the **Despatch** so this paragraph must be brief. She was launched at the Groningen yard of J. Vos & Zoon on 9 February 1931 and delivered to Jan Beck as **Atlas** on 12 May. In 1937 she was sold within the Netherlands and renamed **Despatch**. In May 1940 she was requisitioned by the British Admiralty and manned by a Royal Navy crew. She was used in Operation Dynamo to evacuate allied troops from Dunkirk and then fulfilled the same role of evacuation but from Le Havre in Operation Cycle. In September 1940 she was time chartered for five years by the Ministry of Shipping and later Ministry of Transport. A sale in 1951 saw Kamp's become managers, being replaced by Carebeka six years later. Gruno took over management in 1964. She is unique in this book in having been managed by three of the big management companies. In the meantime, tragedy had befallen the ship on 4 April 1961 when the captain's 4-year-old daughter and cook both drowned after falling into the River Thames. She was sold to Captain Peter Herbert, of Bude, in 1969 and remained in his ownership until sold on in 1975. In November of that year she left Southampton bound for Amsterdam. Renamed **Tika**, she stayed there until leaving for the Persian Gulf via Falmouth on 26 March 1976. Nothing further is known. We see her leaving Cardiff on 7 April 1970.

(John Wiltshire)

In the outline history of the **Mount Everest** on page 13, we note that a ship was used as part payment for that coaster. The ship involved was the **Senior**. Also built by Scheepswerf 'Hoogezand' N.V. Jac Bodewes for Christiaan Bakker & Pieter de Wit, of Groningen, and launched as **Corona** on 25 May 1948, the coaster was delivered to her new owners on 28 September. She was handed back to her builder in 1952 and replaced by the **Mount Everest** which had been launched as **Corona**. The shipyard soon found a buyer for the vessel and in January 1953 she was sold to J. Kajuiter, also of Groningen, and was renamed **Senior**. Management was transferred to Wijnne & Barends. After working for her new owner for twenty years, she was sold for breaking up at Viane, a small village near Nieuwerkerk in November 1973. We see her high and dry at Par on 8 August 1971. She was driven by a 4-cylinder Industrie engine of 240bhp.

(the late Peter Townsend, World Ship Photo Library)

Launched on 27 November 1948, it is astonishing that this vessel survived until 1982 in view of the number of mishaps she encountered. A product of the Martenshoek yard of Scheepswerf Voorwaarts v/h E. J. Hijlkema, she was delivered as **Maria S** to Jacob Smith, of Delfzijl, on 25 February 1949. She was only six months old when she required a new crankshaft which was fitted at the Sander shipyard in Delfzijl. This yard also dealt with the propeller damage suffered at Delfzijl in February 1954. The other incidents can only be summarised. She collided with the **Clan Macdonald** off Cuxhaven on 28 January 1959. In late August of that year, she grounded on rocks off Kalajoki (Finland) and almost exactly a year later she grounded in Lake Vänern (Sweden). On 14 February 1962 she collided with a vessel off Delfzijl. It is no wonder that Jacob Smith sold her in August 1962. Bought by a Swedish owner, she was renamed **Florö**. In 1964 she came into British ownership and was renamed **Isle of Harris** by Roderick Cunningham (Scalpay) Co. Ltd., becoming **Benmatt** in 1976. We see her thus in the River Ouse on 19 August 1976. After a sale to Cypriot-flag operators in 1977 she began to trade in the Mediterranean, generally between Limassol and the Lebanon, initially as **My Hope** and from early 1978 as **Esperance**. She sank off Tripoli, Lebanon, in May 1982.

(Laurie Schofield)

The *Rito* was photographed discharging roadstone in the tidal basin at Dover on 6 September 1979. She was launched as *Triton* at G. J. van der Werff's shipyard in Westerbroek on 20 June 1950 and delivered on 20 August to Jacob Beck, of Groningen, with management by Carebeka. With Beck's Scheepvaartkantoor formed in 1957 by Jacob Beck, the ship would obviously then come into that company's management. Her engine was a 5-cylinder Brons of 300bhp. She suffered two serious casualties during her career. On 24 March 1966 there was an explosion in her engine room when she was off IJmuiden. This resulted in a crack in her hull and rudder damage. Four crew members were taken to hospital in IJmuiden, one later dying from his injuries. The coaster was repaired by Amsterdamse Droogdok Mij (Amsterdam Drydock Company). In February 1973, she was sold to K. A. Pack and G. J. Warnes, of Ipswich, and was renamed *Rito*. The second incident occurred on 20 December 1983 when she struck a submerged object off Filey whilst on passage from Ipswich to the River Tyne. Water flooded into her engine room and her crew abandoned the vessel which was towed to Scarborough. She was declared a constructive total loss and sold to shipbreakers in Hull. Breaking up commenced on 24 April 1984 and had been completed by 28 June.

(C J Tabarin)

Launched at the Slikkerveer shipyard of De Groot & van Vliet on 22 August 1951, the **Prinses Wilhelmina** was delivered on 2 November to Geert Dories, of Groningen. Carebeka looked after her management. Her engine was an 8-cylinder Brons of 500nhp. There were two minor recorded incidents in her career. On 25 February 1963, she put into Marseilles when on passage from Fowey to Italy with china clay. Her master, Captain Johan Vleugels, had injured his left arm and hand and needed hospital attention. Then on 20 February 1964, she was involved in a minor collision off Cuxhaven with the German coaster **Ilse Matthiesen**. Neither ship was seriously damaged and both were able to continue their voyages. She was sold in late May 1975 to an owner in Thessaloniki and raised the Greek flag as **Epivate**. Sold on in 1984, she was renamed **Themikstoklis** which was amended to **Themistoklis P** in 1986. A further sale in 1989 saw her become **Sol** under the flag of Honduras. In 2005 she was damaged during a storm at Mersin having been laid up there since 2000. She had been broken up by 2009. We see her approaching Plymouth on 24 September 1971.

(the late Peter Townsend, Ron Baker collection)

The **Westkust** is one of those vessels to have carried many names during her career. She was launched at the van Diepen shipyard in Waterhuizen on 18 November 1950 and delivered as **Westkust** on 2 February 1951 to owners in Rotterdam. She was driven by an 8-cylinder Brons engine of 500bhp. On 9 December 1951, she encountered heavy weather while on passage from Bo'ness to Hamburg and her cargo of coal shifted causing a 40° list. Her crew abandoned ship but one crewman was injured when climbing into the lifeboat sent from Scarborough; he died later in hospital. The trawler **Swanella** towed the abandoned coaster to Hull, earning a salvage payment of £17,000. Sold to Hamburg owners in July 1962, she was renamed **Peter Frese** and subsequent sales within Germany saw her become **Hermann Suhr** in 1964 and **Herm** in 1980. She changed gender in 1982, becoming **Elke R** and then **Kim G** and **Sonia II** still in 1982. In 1983, she transferred to the flag of Gibraltar and was renamed **Royal Wells** but reverted to her original name of **Westkust** in 1984. She was photographed as such at the Parkkade in Rotterdam on 27 May 1984. The year 1985 saw yet another name when she became **Romney Marsh**. There were no further changes of name. After leaving Par for Rotterdam with china clay on 1 April 1986, she suffered water ingress in her engine room. Following grounding on a sandbank for temporary repairs, she was towed to Rotterdam by the tug **Towing Wizard**, arriving on 13 April. Declared a total loss, she was taken to Hendrik Ido Ambacht for breaking up.

(Bernard McCall)

Photographed at Par on 21 March 1971, the **Bonaire** was launched at the Vooruitgang shipyard of Gebr. Suurmeijer on 24 October 1950 and was delivered to Jan Westers and his family in Groningen on 28 December. Management was entrusted to Wijnne & Barends. Power came from a 6-cylinder Industrie engine of 360bhp. After only ten weeks in service, she suffered a serious fire in her engine room on 19 March 1951 when off Start Point during a ballast passage from London to Bayonne. The crew had to abandon ship and were picked up by a Norwegian tanker which took them to Pernis, near Rotterdam. A French trawler named **Tarana** then made fast to the **Bonaire** but had to release the line because of heavy seas. Several other ships arrived to assist the burning **Bonaire** including two Dutch warships, the latter being hampered in firefighting by the crew of the **Tarana** who sought to retain their capture. The fire was eventually extinguished by the former Royal Navy tug **Freebooter** which towed the **Bonaire** to Plymouth. From there the coaster was towed to Capelle a/d IJssel for repair at the Vuyk shipyard. Sold within the Westers family later in 1951, she was sold for breaking in November 1971 and this commenced at Nieuwe Lekkerland on 3 January 1972.

(Terry Nelder)

The *Herta*, arriving at Swansea on 4 July 1970, was built by Gebr. Coops at Hoogezand. Launched on 26 June 1952, she was delivered to captain/owner Jan Mooij on 21 August. Management was the responsibility of Wagenborg's. Power came from a 4-cylinder Industrie engine of 195bhp. She was involved in several incidents during Captain Mooij's ownership. In early April 1954, she was struck by another Dutch coaster when berthed at Wexford and then five years later she suffered severe engine damage off Borkum and had to be towed to Delfzijl for repairs. She was on passage from Karlskrona to Weymouth with timber at the time. On 27 February 1960 she grounded in the Great Belt because of a navigational error and then on 24 November 1965 she grounded in the Ribble estuary when on passage to Preston. She was attended by the Lytham St Annes lifeboat *Sarah Townsend Porritt* which escorted her to Preston after she had refloated. She was sold to Greek owners in April 1972 and was renamed *Panagia Tinoy*, becoming *Graziella* following a sale within Greece in 1975. Four years later she was sold to unidentified Italian owners. Little else is known about the vessel and she was removed from *Lloyd's Register* in 1999.

(John Wiltshire)

A surprising number of vessels in the fleet of Hollandsche Stoomboot Maatschappij were converted to livestock carriers in later life. The *Johanna Buitelaar* was one such example. Powered by an 8-cylinder Werkspoor engine of 1040bhp, she was launched on 13 December 1952 at the Westerbroek yard of E. J. Smit & Zoon and was delivered as *Vechtstroom* to Hollandsche Stoomboot Maatschappij on 11 March 1953. In 1965 she was sold within the Netherlands to an associate company of Vroon's and was renamed *Johanna Buitelaar*. Conversion to a livestock carrier came in 1973 and we see her outward bound in the Clyde estuary in June of that year. In September 1975 she was renamed *Lincoln Express* by another Vroon associated company. On 11 May 1982 she arrived under tow at Hendrik Ido Ambacht for breaking up.

(John Wiltshire collection)

Outward bound from Swansea in June 1979, the **Pirola** is one of the few coasters in this book to retain the same name throughout her career. She was launched at the Gebr. Niestern shipyard in Delfzijl on 26 November 1952 and delivered to a group of owners based in Delfzijl on 2 April 1953. W. F. Kampman took over management of the ship in 1955 but a decade later management was transferred to Carebeka. Power came from a 6-cylinder Brons engine of 375bhp but in May 1967 this was replaced by a 6-cylinder Stork engine of 395bhp. A sale in 1976 saw her move from the Dutch flag to that of Panama and management switched to Wagenborg but she continued to trade in northern Europe. Her end came in 1980. On 21 May, fire broke out when she was off Colonsay during a voyage from Ballina to Corpach. Her crew was taken off by helicopter and the coaster was towed to Cairnryan by the survey ship HMS **Hydra**. Beyond economical repair, she was sold for breaking up at Cairnryan and this was completed by February 1981.

(Bernard McCall collection)

Photographed at Hayle in May 1969, the **Arneborg** was to prove an unlucky vessel. She entered the water at the Gebr. Sander shipyard in Delfzijl on 12 April 1954 and was delivered as **Tukker** to owners based in Hengelo on 16 June. Management was in the hands of Wagenborg throughout her career. Power came from a 4-cylinder Brons engine of 200bhp. The first crisis came on 12 February 1962 when she grounded on the south-east coast of Sweden during a heavy south-westerly storm whilst on passage from Åhus to Delfzijl with a cargo of timber. Salvage of the vessel was entrusted to a Stockholm-based company. After leaks in the engine-room were plugged with cement, the **Tukker** was towed to Simrishamn a week later. Then on 7 March the **Tukker** was towed to the de Groot & van Vliet shipyard in Slikkerveer for repair. She eventually re-entered service on 5 June.

Three days later, Wagenborg took over ownership. Then in late April 1964, she was renamed **Arneborg** during annual survey at Harlingen. On 3 December 1964, the **Arneborg** lost part of her deck cargo of timber during a storm when 50 miles north of Terschelling. The nine-strong crew were able partially to correct the heavy list by jettisoning more deck cargo and adjusting the ballast. She continued her voyage to Rotterdam at half speed and monitored by the British cargo ship **Flintshire**. The next incident was to prove the final one. When berthed at Dordrecht on 3 March 1973 she was struck by a barge and suffered severe stern damage. She was towed to Delfzijl and declared a constructive total loss. In April 1974 she was sold for breaking up at Hendrik Ido Ambacht.

(John Wiltshire collection)

11

Launched on 7 November 1953 at the Bodewes shipyard in Martenshoek, this coaster was delivered as **Pacific** to Cornelis Tammes, of Groningen, on 12 January 1954. Her engine was an 8-cylinder Brons of 500bhp. In June 1955 she left Europe after being taken on time charter by Westley Shipping in New Orleans but returned four years later after the bankruptcy of the charterers. On 11 December 1961, she was acquired by the Nieuwe Noord Nederlandse shipyard in Groningen as the deposit for a new **Pacific** ordered by Captain Tammes. The shipyard sold her on 19 December 1961 to Telje Albertus Belstra, of Groningen, whose coaster **Wiema**

had sunk nine days previously. Her new owner renamed her **Mari Ann** and handed management to Wagenborg. She left northern Europe for the Mediterranean after purchase in 1975 by Greek owners who renamed her **Marianna**. We see her thus at Paros on 12 April 1987. She remained in Greek ownership for the rest of her career, later becoming **Fotini** (1992), **Odysseus** (1993), and **Iason** (1994). Her eventual fate is unknown although one source suggests she was still trading in mid-2014.

(Neil Burns)

Seen at Plymouth on 14 August 1966, the **Mount Everest** is one of those comparatively few coasters that seems to have had a career with very few noteworthy incidents. She was built at the Martenshoek yard of Bodewes Scheepswerven (Gebr. G. & H. Bodewes) and was launched on 18 March 1954. She was delivered to Christiaan Bakker & Pieter de Wit, of Groningen, on 4 May and was managed by Carebeka. Her engine was an 8-cylinder Brons of 500bhp. The owners' previous coaster **Corona**, built in 1948, was returned to the builder in 1952 and used as part payment for the **Mount Everest** which had in fact been laid down as **Corona**. The only incident worth recording occurred on 4 February 1964 when she grounded on the Danish coast near Guldborgsund when approaching the end of a voyage from Basse Indre to Nykøbing (Falster). In August 1971 she was sold to German owners and converted to a hopper dredger but without change of name. Her only change of identity came in 1974 when she was acquired by Polish owners in Gdansk and renamed **Meduza**. She was broken up at Gdansk in May 1985.

(Terry Nelder)

Launched at the Amels shipyard in Makkum on 12 March 1954, the **Rien Teekman** was delivered to captain/owner Jan Teekman on 29 April following successful trials on the IJsselmeer. Her engine was a 6-cylinder Brons of 375bhp and, unusually, was installed prior to launch. Other members of the captain's family became part owners in future years but management remained with Wagenborg until the ship left Teekman ownership in mid-August 1973. On 16 April 1955, the local newspaper "Friese Koerier" had featured a lengthy article about life on board the ship for the captain's wife, Mrs L. Teekman-Dekker and their three children. Bought by Panamanian-flag operators, the ship was renamed **Esperanza II** but she did not survive much longer. On 4 February 1974 she left Lisbon with a cargo of ammunition and other goods destined for Apapa-Lagos. She reported propeller problems on the following day but nothing further was heard from the ship or her crew. We see the coaster in Millbay Dock, Plymouth, on 14 March 1972. The silo in the background was built in the early 1940s and remained in use for forty years. It later served as a useful windbreak for Brittany Ferries vessels which then used the berth but it was demolished in early 2008.

(the late Peter Townsend, Ron Baker collection)

It is hard to believe that the two vessels on this page are one and the same. Designed for trading to Paris, the **Aiglon** was launched at the Westerbroek shipyard of J. G. Bröerken on 2 April 1955 and delivered as **Gironde** on 3 June to a single ship company in which Kamp's had a 97% share. Not surprisingly, Kamp's acted as managers of the ship. Power came from a 6-cylinder MAN engine of 300bhp. In September 1965 she was sold to a Rotterdam owner by whom she was transferred to Beck's management and two months later she was renamed **Aiglon**. In this view though, we see her as a museum ship in Rotterdam on 11 May 1999. The career that took her there is outlined in the caption below.

(Stan Tedford)

After trading for almost a decade as **Aiglon**, a change of identity came in July 1976 when a sale within the Netherlands saw her become **Willy-B** and a switch to management by Wijnne & Barends. We see her as such in the RIver Ouse on 22 June 1983. Her name was amended to **Willy** in 1984. She remained trading in northern Europe although sold to a Maltese company in 1985 when she was renamed **Dawn**, becoming **Dawn Sky** two years later. On 20 December 1987 she arrived in Rotterdam from Keadby with machinery damage and was laid up. There was also an allegation of involvement in smuggling and the coaster was handed over to the Netherlands government. On 2 May 1990, now once again named **Aiglon**, she arrived at Hendrik Ido Ambacht for breaking up but was later bought for restoration as a museum ship and was berthed in the Coolhaven in Rotterdam from 1999. On 28 July 2003, she arrived at a breaker's yard in 's Gravendeel and breaking up began on 6 October 2003.

(David Gallichan)

The **Bram** was launched at the Westerbroek shipyard of G. J. van der Werff on 29 October 1955 and was completed by the end of the year, the owners being a small group of businessmen in Groningen. Power came from a 6-cylinder Brons engine of 395bhp. The first incident in her career occurred on 1 July 1960 when she suffered some damage after colliding with the Shell tanker **Kabylia** in the Manchester Ship Canal. On 23 March 1966 she grounded 20 miles west of Cape Episel, Portugal, while on passage from England to Lisbon and Huelva; she was refloated by an unidentified tug. Also in 1966 Carebeka took over her management and remained as managers until she was sold within the Netherlands six years later. We see her arriving at Cardiff on 11 July 1971. She remained in Dutch ownership until 1977 when she was bought by owners in Iran and renamed **Armaghan**. Further sales in the Middle East saw her become **Al Toufiq** in 1980 and then **Taisir** in 1986. She was removed from *Lloyd's Register* in 1996 and her ultimate fate is unknown.

(John Wiltshire)

Just passing the western breakwater as she left Swansea on 24 April 1969, the **Albert V** was one of several ships built and owned in the Netherlands but managed by International Shipbrokers Ltd in London. She was launched at the Niestern shipyard in Delfzijl on 26 April 1955 and delivered on 13 July. She was driven by a 4-cylinder Industrie engine of 395bhp. In October 1975 she was sold to James Henry Ramagge who transferred her to the Panamanian flag as **Ramblas**. A further sale in 1978 saw her renamed **Prim**. Her career as such was to prove short-lived as she sank on 21 April 1979 when ten miles south of Figueira da Foz when on passage from that port to Casablanca. Her crew was rescued.

(John Wiltshire)

The **Jo** was one of those coasters that had an interesting career which actually began with her construction. She was the last complete vessel to be built at the Wirdum shipyard of A. Apol, the builder subsequently moving to Appingedam and trading as Scheepswerf Appingedam v/h A. Apol. Part of the **Thalassa**, the first vessel to be built at the Appingedam yard, had in fact been constructed at Wirdum. Launched on 28 May 1955, the **Jo** was originally named **Kars** and was delivered to Groningen-based Harm Peter Veling on 4 August. The first incident occurred on 15 October 1963 when three of her crew were arrested in Copenhagen for smuggling alcohol and cigarettes. The authorities had been informed by a jealous young Danish lady, aware of the smuggling, who had been jilted by one of the Dutch sailors. Three years later the ship was lengthened by six metres at Alblasserdam. Between July and December 1967 she was renamed **Superior Trader**, one of several coasters chartered for a thrice-weekly service between Scheveningen and Great Yarmouth. From that service eventually emerged Norfolk Line. Sold and renamed **Jo** in 1970, we see her approaching Selby on 18 May 1980. She sailed out to the Caribbean in late 1985 and was removed from *Lloyd's Register* in 1998. In 1972 her original 6-cylinder Werkspoor engine of 395bhp was replaced by a 6-cylinder Kelvin of 320bhp.

(Neil Burns)

17

The **Maria Teresa** was launched at the Gebr. van Diepen yard in Waterhuizen on 2 July 1955 and delivered as **Oceaan** to Roelf Tamme Tammes, of Groningen, on 2 September. Her engine was a 6-cylinder Werkspoor of 820bhp. She was reported to be the first Groningen owned coaster to be fitted with radar - a Decca 212 model. After fourteen years service, she was sold to an Italian owner based in Naples and was renamed **Maria Teresa**. She seems to have had an incident-free career. In late 1979 she was laid up at Baia, near Naples, and in heavy weather on the night of 20/21 December 1979 she broke her moorings and ran aground. She was deemed unworthy of repair and was scrapped locally in March 1981. She was photographed at the port of Heraklion in Crete in May 1973.

(John Wiltshire collection)

Powered by an 8-cylinder Industrie engine of 600bhp, the **Medusa** was launched at the Bodewes Scheepswerven yard in Martenshoek on 30 July 1955 and delivered as **Rubato** to Derk Schothorst and Wietze Schuitema, of Groningen, on 26 September. Management was in the hands of Carebeka until she was sold to a Rotterdam-based owner in mid-July 1970, being renamed **Medusa**. She left northern Europe in 1974 when acquired by a Greek owner and renamed **Evangelos**. Later sales within Greece saw her renamed **Manolis K** (1981), **Michalis G** (1982) and **Doralia** (1988). She is thought to have been sold for breaking up in September 2003. We see her leaving Plymouth on 30 March 1973. The white dust on her hull is an almost certain indication that she has loaded china clay.

(the late Peter Townsend, World Ship Photo Library)

Launched as **Ella** by Scheepsbouw Unie at Groningen on 20 November 1954, this coaster was the first of two sisterships that had very similar early careers. Sister vessel **Vlieree** appeared in *Coasters of the 1950s*. Our subject was delivered on 10 February 1955 but prior to that, on 15 December, she was renamed **Marianne** and the name **Ella** was given to her sister. Both were intended for trading to Paris for the Swedish Götha Line and this explains their distinctive low air draught design. They carried steel, rails and paper on the southbound voyage and returned with Renault and Citroën cars. The **Marianne** had an 8-cylinder MaK engine of 700bhp. Replaced by more modern vessels in the mid-1960s, she was sold within the Netherlands and renamed **Vliehors** in March 1966. She was soon trading more widely and grounded at Kingston, Jamaica, on 5 July 1968 as she tried to leave the port unassisted during a strike by pilots. We see her in the River Mersey on 18 April 1979. In late January 1981, she arrived at Harlingen from Sharpness and was laid up along with her sister. In early 1982, both vessels were sold for conversion to dredgers. The **Vlieree** was indeed converted but the **Vliehors** remained at Harlingen for a further ten years. In 1992, all her upperworks were removed and she was converted to a crane barge and later used as a floating wharf at the Welgelegen shipyard in Harlingen. She was eventually broken up in November 2001.

(David Gallichan)

Despite passing through the hands of several owners, the *Wegro* retained her original name from her launch at Foxhol on 5 February 1955 until she was broken up at Queenborough in mid-1985. Driven by a 6-cylinder Brons engine of 395bhp, she was delivered to Juko Wester, of Groningen, on 7 April 1955. Management was initially with Wijnne & Barends but was transferred to Carebeka in 1962. Two years prior to that she had rescued 16 crew members from a Swedish vessel that had collided with a BP tanker in dense fog off the Swedish island of Juist. She hoisted the Irish flag in October 1971. In late April 1981, she was involved in an incident of her own. She was approaching Great Yarmouth to collect a cargo of grain for Ghent but gale force winds prevented her from entering and the master decided to ride out the storm at anchor. Her anchors proved ineffective and even with her engines full astern, the ship could not prevent grounding. Two boys enjoying a holiday on board, aged 12 and 15, were rescued by the Gorleston Coast Rescue Company,

the first time its services had been needed for over twenty years. Eventually a channel had to be dug in the sand to get the ship back to water. Whilst this work was ongoing, the ship was opened to the public for guided tours, the proceeds being donated to the RNLI. On 1 May, the Yarmouth tug *Hector Read* failed in an attempt to tow the coaster back to sea but was more successful on the next day when the Alexandra tug *Indomitable* provided more assistance. On 18 August 1984 she suffered a broken crankshaft whilst on passage from Montrose to Ghent. She was towed to Grimsby on the next day and three weeks later was towed to Queenborough. In November 1984 she was declared a compromised total loss and was sold for breaking up locally. This began in July 1985 but was not completed until February 1988. She was photographed in the lock at Sharpness on 4 October 1979.

(Cedric Catt)

Launched on 22 June 1956, this coaster had the distinction of being the first one built at the new shipyard of Gebr. Sander in Delfzijl. On 10 September 1956, she was delivered as **Stortemelk** to Lammert Schothorst, of Hoogezand, and Johannes Elias Houwerzijl, of Groningen. Management was looked after by Gruno. Her engine was a 6-cylinder Industrie of 395bhp. After three years in Dutch ownership she was sold on 19 December 1959 to a Swedish owner and was renamed **Ranskär**. She passed through the hands of two other Swedish owners without renaming before being acquired in early February 1974 by Roderick Cunningham (Scalpay) Co Ltd. She then was renamed **Isle of Rona** and we see her on 8 July 1976 as she left Gladstone Lock at Liverpool at the start of a voyage to Belfast with a cargo of grain loaded in Royal Seaforth Dock. A sale to West Country Shipping Limited saw her become **Barnstaple Trader** in 1981. The year 1983 began badly for her. On 17 January she suffered damage at Ghent when severe gusts of wind caused her to contact a bulk carrier whilst shifting berth. Then on 24 February she was arrested at Inverness as a result of a claim by a former master for wages and other money owed. Current crew members were also owed back wages. On 17 March, she was struck by the small passenger vessel **Scot II** whilst laid up at Inverness. She did not trade again. On 26 July 1984 she was sold at auction to Liguria Maritime for breaking at the company's yard in Kent.

(Neil Burns)

21

The **Margriet Anja** proved to be one of the coasters that was involved in several minor incidents during her career. She was built by C. Amels Zoon at the Welgelegen shipyard in Makkum. Launched on 24 March 1956, she was delivered to her Groningen-based owner on 22 May. Power came from a 6-cylinder MWM engine of 750bhp. Her first reported incident was on 10 July 1959 when she grounded whilst on passage from Horsens to Rotterdam with a cargo of malt. Then on 1 March 1960 she suffered minor damage when hit by the German coaster **Diana** (1585gt/56) when moored to a buoy at Greenhithe. She struck a railway bridge on the Manchester Ship Canal when leaving Partington on 25 November 1961 and on 25 September 1962 she suffered serious rudder damage after grounding on rocks near Säbbskär in Finland. Initially management was with

Kamp's but transferred to Gruno after a sale to a partnership based in Harlingen in May 1969. Her misfortunes continued, however. On 19 February 1970 she reported serious engine damage on passage from Pasajes to Antwerp and was towed to Bilbao where repairs lasted almost 3 months. Then on 1 November 1972, she had camshaft problems necessitating eventual replacement. She left northern Europe in June 1975 following purchase by Piraeus-based owners who renamed her **Apollonia IV**. A sale to owners in Thessaloniki saw her become **Vera** in 1983. Her ending was almost inevitable. She grounded on a reef near Lefteris on the island of Skiathos. She was abandoned by her crew and, with a huge gash in her hull, heeled over. We see her in Millbay Docks, Plymouth, on 7 May 1972.

(Terry Nelder)

Until her final demise, the **Jutland** seems to have had a career without major incidents. She was launched at the De Waal shipyard in Zaltbommel on 21 March 1953 and delivered in late July to Berend Bosma and Jan Kuipers, nominally of Groningen although the latter was a ship's agent in Denmark. Wijnne & Barends looked after the management of the ship. She had an 8-cylinder Brons engine of 500bhp. In 1978 she was sold to Cypriot owners and renamed **Apollon**. Further sales within Cyprus saw her become **Al Rayes** (1979), **Bader T** (1981) and **Arkan I** (1983). On 21 April 1984, when on passage from Limassol to Tripoli (Lebanon) with 31 containers, 11 crew and 15 passengers, she sank in Vassiliko Bay. One passenger drowned and the others were taken back to Limassol. She was photographed when outward bound from Swansea on 20 November 1970.

(John Wiltshire)

23

The **Valerie B**, photographed at Par on 11 August 1973, had an astonishingly short career under the Dutch flag. It lasted only five weeks. She was launched as **Spolesto** on 26 November 1955 at the Groningen yard of Noord-Nederlandsche Scheepswerven and delivered on 18 January 1956 to owners Spoorhout N.V., of The Hague, with management by Rotterdam-based Dammers & van der Heide. On 22 February she was acquired by Zillah Shipping Ltd and was renamed **Edgefield**. Nine years later, she hoisted the Irish flag when bought by Marine Transport Services Ltd, of Cork, by whom she was renamed **Sarsfield**. In 1970, she returned to British ownership, becoming **Valerie B**. The 1970s saw her pass through the hands of several British owners, being renamed **Rosemary D** (1973), **Silloth Trader** (1974) and **Radcliffe Trader** (1979). As such she was laid up in Barry on 1 September 1982, eventually sailing on 25 March 1983 to Rotterdam following a sale to a Dutch owner by whom she was renamed **Mirabelle** under the Panamanian flag. She later sailed to the Caribbean. On 2 March 1984 she struck a submerged object off Goajira, Colombia while on passage from Aruba to Cartagena. Four days later she was declared a constructive total loss and was subsequently broken up.

(the late Peter Townsend, Ron Baker collection)

The Martenshoek shipyard of Hijlkema & Zoon launched the **Corona** on 1 December 1956 and on 30 January of the following year, the coaster was delivered to a partnership of two brothers based in Delfzijl. Management was entrusted to Carebeka. Driven by a 4-cylinder Brons engine of 220bhp, she was sold to a company in Gibraltar in May 1974 and was renamed **Mini May**, becoming **Palmetta** the following year after a sale to owners in Panama. On 18 September 1978 she foundered when eight miles south-east of Cat Island in the Bahamas.

(the late Peter Townsend, Ron Baker collection)

Launched by Arnhemsche Scheepsbouw Maatschappij on 22 June 1957, this vessel was delivered as **Vliestroom** to Hollandsche Stoomboot Maatschappij on 19 September. She was the fourth vessel to carry this name for her owners. She was driven by an 8-cylinder Werkspoor engine of 1040bhp and had accommodation for two passengers. After 12 years trade as an open shelterdeck vessel, she was sold to Vroon's, of Breskens, and in 1970 went to the Cassens shipyard in Emden where she was converted to a livestock carrier. Named **Frisian Express**, ownership passed through various Vroon subsidiary companies over the next fifteen years. In the mid-1980s, she was trading mainly between Sète and Tunis. She arrived at Sète on 21 December 1987 and was laid up awaiting repairs. No repair took place and she was delivered to Vigo on 17 August 1989 for breaking which began two months later. She is seen outward bound in the Clyde estuary in June 1969.

(John Wiltshire collection)

Photographed at Swansea on 28 September 1973, the **Lerwick Trader** was launched on 21 November 1956 at the D. & J. Boot's 'De Vooruitgang' shipyard at Alphen aan den Rijn. Named **Henriette B**, she was delivered on 24 January 1957 to Gerrit Brijder, of Heemstede. She came into British ownership in early January 1964 when bought by Hay & Co, of Lerwick. Renamed **Shetland Trader**, she was managed by W. N. Lindsay Ltd, of Leith. With another vessel bought in early 1972 and to be renamed **Shetland Trader**, she became **Shetland Trader 1** before becoming **Lerwick Trader** in February 1972. She was renamed **Hoxa Sound** after sale to William Dennison, of Kirkwall, in 1979. Later renamed **Telebar**, she was deleted from *Lloyd's Register* in 2001 as her continued existence was doubtful. There were two incidents in her career. In summer 1958, when at anchor in the River Thames, she was hit by a tanker whose steering gear had failed. She was taken to Harlingen, arriving on 5 August 1958 and repairs being completed on 7 October. In the following year, she listed 30° to port while on passage from Dundalk to the Mediterranean. After a 4-day tow to Brest it was discovered that her cargo of copper ore had liquefied, thus causing the list.

(John Wiltshire)

Although there have been many notable fleets of French cargo vessels, these have always comprised large ocean-going ships rather than coasters. During the 1960s, however, some Dutch coasters were acquired and became frequent visitors to ports in the south of England. The **Côte de Grace** was built at the Kramer & Booy shipyard in Kootstertille as **Mutatie** for a partnership of three based in Groningen to whom she was handed over on 29 August 1957 having been launched on 6 July. Her engine was a 6-cylinder MWM of 500bhp. She was renamed **Côte de Grace** following her sale to France in 1965. We see her leaving Swansea on 1 June 1971. Later changes of names saw her become **Santa Manza** (1972), **Tergit** (1979), and **Salvadora** (1981). Later in 1981 she was purchased by a Moroccan company, Société des Ciments du Sahara, and renamed **Zahra**. It seems likely that she was working in the cement trade. At some time in the 1990s, she stranded about 10 miles (16km) from Sidi Ifni on the Atlantic coast of Morocco. The wreck was still upright in 2012.

(John Wiltshire)

Powered by a 4-cylinder Brons engine of 220bhp, the **Jacob Teekman** arrives at Swansea on 27 May 1970. She was launched at the Friesland shipyard in Lemmer on 13 July 1957. Owner/captain Jan Teekman had a three-fifths share in the vessel which was named after his twelve-year-old son who performed the naming ceremony and launch. The launch itself did not pass off smoothly - there was a fifteen minute wait for the ship to move down the slipway after the naming. The Friesland yard had opened in October 1956 and although it had built three smaller vessels, this was its first coaster and a further seven were on order. The **Jacob Teekman** was delivered to the Teekman family on 3 October 1957. The only incident of note in her career occurred only a few weeks after delivery when she grounded on the Swedish coast in late November 1957 following a navigational error. Her name was modified to **Jaco** in 1974. Although sold to Panamanian flag operators in 1977, she continued to trade in northern Europe as **Irene-S** and indeed when sold and renamed **Sylvia Anna** in 1981. Becoming **Gisela** in 1983 she eventually left northern Europe and on 6 April 1984 was noted leaving Singapore bound for Bombay, arriving on 21 May and remaining there for at least six months. Sold and renamed **Sea Power** in early 1985, she disappeared from movement reports after leaving Haldia (Calcutta) on 6 April 1985.

(John Wiltshire)

The **Johanca** proved to be another Dutch coaster whose final years are shrouded in mystery. Launched at the Gebr. Coops shipyard in Hoogezand on 17 September 1957, she was delivered to Klaas and D. Veenma, of Groningen, on 28 November. Management was in the hands of Wijnne & Barends. Her 6-cylinder Brons engine of 395bhp gave her a speed of 9.5 knots. On 8 June 1968, she suffered severe engine problems when 40 miles south of the Smalls Lighthouse and was towed to Dublin. Several days later she was towed from Dublin to the Sander shipyard at Delfzijl where a new 6-cylinder Brons engine was fitted. After a brief period under the Isle of Man flag in 1974, she was bought by owners in Sharjah and renamed **Alfajer II** in 1975. She was renamed **Golden Star** in 1976 and then, under Panamanian registry, **Al Amena** in 1978. She became **Vaseem** in 1987 and was seen under this name at Karachi in May of that year. We see her reflected in the still waters of Millbay Dock, Plymouth. on 3 December 1972.

(the late Peter Townsend, World Ship Photo Library)

A feature of Dutch coaster (and barge) naming has always been an eagerness to use Latin words and phrases. **Navigare** is the Latin verb meaning "to sail". The ship was built by Scheepswerf Hoogezand N.V. Jac Bodewes at Bergum. Launched on 30 March 1957, she was delivered as **Tubo** on 14 June to Willem Bootsman, of Delfzijl, with management by W. Kampman, of Amsterdam. She was renamed **Moerdijk** for a time charter to Rotterdam-based Solleveld & Van der Meer in 1961/62. In late September 1969, the Kampman company took over ownership of the coaster and renamed her **Navigare** a year later. She was photographed in East Waterloo Dock, Liverpool, on 5 January 1976. She retained the name **Navigare** when bought by operators in the Cayman Islands in 1978. Trading in the Caribbean for various owners, she became **Paramount C** in 1982, **Eagle I** in 1986, **Navigare** in 1991 and **Paramount C** in 1993. One source suggests that she was still in service in 2006 but she had been removed from *Lloyd's Register* by 2009.

(Neil Burns)

The **Vedette** was launched at the Bodewes shipyard in Martenshoek on 26 March 1957 and was delivered to Beck's Scheepvaartkantoor in Groningen on 14 July. Her 8-cylinder Brons engine of 650bhp gave her a service speed of 11 knots, appreciably faster than many other coasters of her generation. She was acquired by Swedish brothers Petter and Solve Pettersson and renamed **Westbris** in September 1962. She became **Rigina** in 1976 when sold to Ingemar Gudmundsson, of Gävle. He remained as beneficial owner following a further sale to his overseas company in 1988. The coaster was laid up at Horsens in Denmark between May and September 2002, and again between those same months in 2003. During those periods, the ship was manned only by the Ukrainian mate and her watchdog. In early 2008 it was reported that she had been sold to a Belgian businessman who planned to convert her to a music studio with accommodation for musicians. The sale was never completed and she was sold later in that year for further trade in the Caribbean. She is understood to be still trading as **Rigina** under the flag of Guyana. We see her at Fort de France on 10 March 2011 with Beck's characteristic letter B still used on her funnel.

(Yvon Perchoc)

At this point we take temporary leave of our chronological sequence in order to concentrate on a group of thirteen coasters that have been considered to be the acme of the classic Dutch coaster. Nine of the group were ordered by Wagenborg for their own account and four for private owners with Wagenborg as commercial managers. With a gross tonnage of just under 400 and a deadweight of approximately 525 tonnes, they were not as big as some coasters then being built. The *Spaarneborg,* seen leaving Swansea on 30 April 1969, was the second of the thirteen classic coasters to be delivered. Launched at the Amels shipyard in Makkum on 21 September 1957, she was delivered to Wagenborg on 30 October following successful trials on the IJsselmeer that day. Her main engine was a 4-cylinder Werkspoor of 220bhp. Her career had a bad start. Before entering commercial service she collided with a dredger in Harlingen.

(John Wiltshire)

After fifteen years in the Wagenborg fleet, the *Spaarneborg* was sold to owners in Rotterdam and renamed *La Paloma*. In 1975, she was bought by a Jersey-based company and renamed *Cantium*. In 1979, she became *Sheila Maria* and retained this name despite several changes of ownership varying between Jersey and Gibraltar. In late 1984, it was reported that she had been sold and was to be renamed *Falabella* but that never happened. On 11 May 1985 she left Douala with Selby as her destination. She suffered machinery problems and was towed to Dakar where she arrived on 3 June. Nothing more is known about her but she was not removed from *Lloyd's Register* until 1999. We see her as *Cantium* at Liverpool, on 18 May 1978.

(Neil Burns)

Rather than constantly referring back to this group over the next twenty pages or so, we are grouping them together with one exception, namely the final one delivered in 1964 and seen on page 58. The hull of the coaster seen here was built at the Friesland shipyard in Lemmer with completion at the Welgelegen yard of C. Amels Zoon in Makkum. She was handed over to Wagenborg as *Lingeborg* on 29 March 1960. She retained Wagenborg management when sold and renamed *Farel* in late January 2001. She was photographed at Runcorn on 4 April 1976.

(Neil Burns)

In February 1978 the *Farel* was renamed *Ceol Mor* when acquired by an Irvine company. We see her at Ardrossan on 19 July 1983. Her original engine was a 4-cylinder Brons of 224bhp but this was replaced in 1981 with a 6-cylinder Cummins of 365bhp. In 1983 she was sold to owners in Nassau, Bahamas, and left Southampton for Nassau on 30 September 1983. Later named *Lady Lotmore*, she became *Lady L'Belle* in 1996 when bought by owners in Malabo, Equatorial Guinea. No longer mentioned in movement reports, her area of trade at that time is unknown. However, she was suspected of drug smuggling by the authorities in Venezuela during 2000/2001 and was abandoned at Puerto Cabello. There she remained derelict and partially capsized in 2014.

(Alastair Paterson)

The **Margreet** is another of the thirteen coasters built for ownership by Wagenborg. We see her at Gloucester on 18 May 1979. Launched at the Friesland shipyard in Lemmer on 3 December 1960, she was delivered as **Schieborg** to the Wagenborg company on 10 January of the following year. Power came from a 4-cylinder Brons engine of 224bhp. Sold to Egbert Jan Potkamp in April 1972, she was renamed **Bonny** and became **Margreet** when bought by Gerrit Broere in September 1976. Both owners retained Wagenborg management. She left northern Europe for the Caribbean in autumn 1983 after being renamed **Mrs White** by an owner in the Virgin Islands. Later changes of name saw her become **Ellenaki** in 1987, **Helena Sea** in 1989 and **Melinda D** in 1997. The only incident of note seems to have been her arrest and subsequent lay-up in the Miami River in 1986. Some sources listed her as still in service in 2012.

(Cedric Catt)

Yet another example of the thirteen sisterships and also built by Scheepswerf Friesland at Lemmer, this coaster was launched on 10 March 1961 and delivered to the Wagenborg company as **Dintelborg** on 25 April. A 4-cylinder Brons engine of 224bhp provided the power. Sold to brothers Geert and Willem Timmer in late June 1975, she was renamed **St Michael** with registry changing from Delfzijl to Groningen; Wagenborg continued as managers. In early February 1978 a sale saw her become **Mieke W** under the flag of Panama and she retained this flag after becoming **Elias-Jr** in 1980. Although in Greek ownership, she continued to trade in northern Europe until Spring 1986 when she moved to the Mediterranean. She left Rochefort for Alexandria via Ceuta on 9 May 1986 and in August she was renamed **Melani**. She had long disappeared from movement reports by the time of the next sale. This was in 1997 when she reverted to her orginal name of **Dintelborg**. Her end came on 20 January 2001 when she stranded on Isla de Margarita in Venezuela and was later abandoned by her owner. She was photographed as **Elias Jr.** in the North Sea Canal on 26 April 1984.

(Bernard McCall collection)

The appearance of some coasters changed quite radically over the years. We now see a member of the standard Wagenborg class without any cargo handling gear. This coaster was launched at the Amels shipyard in Makkum on 10 January 1961 and delivered to Wagenborg as **Delfborg** on 23 February. She was driven by a 4-cylinder Brons engine of 224bhp. She remained in Wagenborg management after sales in 1972 and 1975, her name being changed to **Manta** and **Calvijn** on those occasions. When built she had two 2-tonne derricks but these were removed in the mid-1970s. In 1977, she moved to the Panamanian flag as **Ank** and became **Freetrade** in 1981 initially under the flag of the Isle of Man but then the Maltese flag from 1986. This image of her about to pass beneath the Humber Bridge is undated.

She arrived at Rotterdam from Brightlingsea on 8 September 1988 and was laid up. Subsequently sold, she was renamed **Maya** and departed for the Caribbean in 1990. Later changes of identity saw her become **Misty** (1990), **Pirana** (1991), **Miss Beholden** (1993) and finally **Carmencita** (1995). In March 1993 she stranded on the west coast of Western Sambo Reef after experiencing difficulties whilst on passage from Miami to Progreso with a cargo of cigarettes and chocolates. Later towed off, she was taken to Stock Island, Key West, and laid up there. On 27 June 1996, she left Barranquilla (Colombia) for Chichirivichi (Venezuela). She later foundered and her crew was rescued by the Shell tanker **Euplecta**.

(David Gallichan)

The **Benlow Viking**, seen leaving Cardiff on 24 May 1976, was constructed by Scheepswerf 'Foxhol' v/h Gebr. Muller at Foxhol. Launched on 19 February 1958, she was delivered as **Wijmers** to a consortium of four Groningen-based owners on 17 May. Management was entrusted to Carebeka. In November 1973 she was chartered by Hollandsche Stoomboot Maatschappij and renamed **Vliestroom** to fit in with the naming scheme of the charterer. A sale within the Netherlands saw her become **Viking** in early 1975 and just over one year later she became **Benlow Viking** when bought by St Swithins Shipping Co Ltd. From 1978 she traded as **Lek Viking** under the flag of Singapore before reverting to **Viking** in 1980. Her end was a protracted business. She was arrested off Stromboli, Italy, on 17 March 1984 and was escorted by Italian coastguards to Messina, the allegation being that she was smuggling arms and ammunition. The ship and crew were subsequently released by the Messina Supreme Court but the coaster remained in port. In April 1992 it was eventually sold for scrap but this did not commence until February 1994; breaking up was completed by 26 July 1994.

(John Wiltshire)

The **Antarctica**, powered by a 6-cylinder Deutz engine of 224bhp, was built by v/h Th. J. Fikkers at Foxhol and launched on 7 June 1958 and delivered on 14 August to a Groningen-based partnership by whom her management was entrusted to Wagenborg. This company remained as manager through several sales until 1982 when she hoisted the flag of Panama although still named **Antarctica**. It was not until 1985 that she had a change of identity when she became **Anna-Tica** under the flag of Honduras. She left Antwerp on 28 February 1988 and sailed to the Caribbean and by summer of that year had been renamed **Gene Express** and was trading out of Miami. The same owner seems to have renamed her **Saint Charles** in 1990 and then restored her original name of **Antarctica** two years later. Under new ownership, she became **Martine H** in 2003 but by then had already been removed from *Lloyd's Register* and there is no further news about this vessel. We see her as **Antarctica** at Aberdeen in March 1975.

(Alastair Paterson)

Built at the Jac Bodewes shipyard in Hoogezand, this coaster was launched as **Viod** on 24 October 1957 and delivered to owner Klaas Groen, of IJmuiden, on 7 January 1958. Her engine was a 6-cylinder Brons of 395bhp. Management was in the hands of Wijnne & Barends who became joint owners later in the year. In 1963, in fact, they became sole owners and renamed the ship to **Viola**. We see her approaching the lock at Swansea on 17 February 1970.

(John Wiltshire)

It was in 1973 that the **Viola** was sold to Willem Visser, of Sliedrecht, and she then became **Wilma**. We see her as such as she passes Goole on 27 July 1977. A sale within the Netherlands in 1982 saw her become **Francisca** before reverting to **Viola** in the following year. The sequence of girls' names ended in 1985 when a further sale saw her become **Hermes**. On 6 September 1989 she arrived at Rotterdam from King's Lynn and was laid up. There she remained until mid-July 1992 when she departed to Hendrik Ido Ambacht for repairs. Now sold, she reverted to a girl's name and became **Justine**. With repairs completed by mid-October, she departed for Europoort and then Plymouth, leaving the Devon port on 3 November and sailing via Las Palmas to Kingston, Jamaica, and then trading in the Caribbean. Remaining in the same ownership, she became **Anne J Carida** in 1994 and was removed from *Lloyd's Register* in 2002 as her continued existence was in doubt.

(Neil Burns)

The **Martinistad** was launched at the J. G. Bijlholt shipyard in Foxhol on 21 September 1957 and was delivered on 9 January of the following year. Power came from a 6-cylinder Deutz engine of 400nhp. Some sources suggest that she was initially under Wagenborg management, moving to Gruno in 1960; others claim she was under Gruno management from the start. In mid-August 1971 she was bought by British owners and was renamed **Dolphin G**. On 13 January 1972 she was escorted into Cowes by the tug **Fairplay X** when she suffered a 10° list to port whilst on passage from London to Spain. The list had been caused by leaks in her double bottom tanks. Sold on in 1973, her name was modified to **Dolphin City** but she became **Hootern** in mid-1974 when managed by R Lapthorn. In September 1976 she entered the fleet of General Freight and was renamed **River Taw**. On 9 August 1979 she again suffered a leak when off Stepper Point and she was towed to Padstow the following day. Later in the year she was sold for trading in the Caribbean. On 8 September 1981, she stranded on a reef off St Kitts during a tropical storm. She was refloated with tug assistance and taken to Martinique for temporary repairs. Some reports claim she was then sunk as an artificial reef; others suggest she foundered in 1984. We see her at Newport on 13 February 1971.

(John Wiltshire)

A 6-cylinder Brons engine of 395bhp powered the **Pandora** which was launched at the Westerbroek shipyard of G. J. van der Werff on 6 February 1958. On 4 April she was delivered to Harm Westers, of Groningen, with management in the hands of Kampman. In October 1962 she was sold to a partnership of three, one of whom was Willem Frederik Kampman himself and his company took over ownership in late January 1970. She was photographed soon after leaving Goole on 15 May 1977. In late August 1977 she was sold to a company based in Abu Dhabi but she still retained her original name. Indeed she was noted at Karachi as **Pandora** in August 1978. Her first change of name seems to have occurred in 1980 when a sale to another owner based in Abu Dhabi saw her become **Al Sahara**. Laid up at Abu Dhabi in 2004, she is understood to have sunk there in February 2005 but was later raised and returned to lay up. She was seen in June 2007 with the name **Soroosh** painted on her bow.

(David Gallichan)

Built by E. J. Smit & Zoon at Westerbroek, this vessel was launched on 10 June 1958 and delivered as **Libertas** to Amsterdam-based Nieuwe Kustvaart Maatschappij on 16 September. The ship's operators were Koninklijke Nederlandsche Stoomboot Maatschappij (KNSM) - The Royal Netherlands Steamship Company on 28 August. Power came from a 6-cylinder Werkspoor engine of 750bhp. KNSM continued to manage the ship following sale in December 1972 to Cypriot-flag owners by whom she was renamed **Berta**. Management ceased following a sale within Cyprus in November 1973, as a result of which she was renamed **Croesus**. Initially registered at Famagusta, this changed to Limassol following the division of Cyprus in the following year. Then in 1975 she was sold to operators in Lebanon and renamed **Rabunion V**. Lloyd's Register notes that she was converted to a livestock carrier in 1982 and this information is repeated elsewhere, presumably following Lloyd's. Almost certainly she was converted prior to that date as her owners specialised in the carriage of livestock and would not have left her unconverted for seven years. It is probable that Lloyd's were not informed of the conversion until 1982. She was sold and renamed **Amro-Z** in 1992 and was thus named when photographed at Dubai on 16 February 2001. The ship arrived at Mumbai for breaking up in late April 2003.

(Roger Hurcombe)

It has become commonplace for the hull of a ship to be built in one yard and the vessel completed in another. In the late 1950s, it was less common. The hull of this coaster was built at the Antwerp yard of C. Meyntjes & Zoon with completion by De Groot & van Vliet at Slikkerveer. She was delivered as **Ank-T** on 11 June 1959 to owners in Zaandam. A decade later she was acquired by Hendrik Buitenkamp in Groningen who entrusted management to Wijnne & Barends and renamed the vessel **Maritta Johanna**. During November and December 1972 she had seven tanks fitted in her hold for the carriage of bulk cement. This work was done at the Niestern shipyard in Groningen. We see her leaving Aberdeen in July 1974. Not only was she sold and renamed **Riet** later in 1974 but also her original 8-cylinder Deutz engine of 530bhp was replaced by a more powerful 660bhp Deutz engine. In November 1974 she was sold yet again and was now renamed **Mercurius**, this being amended to **BC Mercurius** after purchase by Blue Circle Industries in 1988. Four years prior to that, she was fitted with yet another new engine, this being a 12-cylinder Caterpillar of 740bhp. On 21 October 1988 she had a fire in her engine room when on passage from Stornoway to Larne. Later declared a total loss, she was towed to Garston for breaking up.

(Alastair Paterson)

Launched by Scheepswerf "Friesland" at Lemmer, the **Batavier V** was delivered to Wm. H. Müller on 29 January 1959. Her main engine was an 8-cylinder MAN of 1680bhp. The Müller company was established in Düsseldorf on 18 April 1876 and a Dutch office opened in Rotterdam on 3 June 1878. On 1 November 1895, the company took over Nederlandsche Stoomboot Maatschappij along with its fleet and passenger/cargo service to London. With all the ships working on this service named "Batavier" followed by a numeral, it became known as the Batavier Line. In 1958 the passenger service to London was stopped, only the freight service continued and lasted until 1971 when all the ships including **Batavier V** were taken over by Scheepvaartbedrijf Kroonburgh N.V., Rotterdam, and all the shipping activities were ended in 1972. Although the style of the owning company changed over the years, the **Batavier V** did not receive a new name until sold to Cypriot-flag owners in autumn 1976 when she became **Satellite**. Keeping the same name, she was bought by a company in Doha, Qatar, in 1982 and, following a further sale, converted to a livestock carrier in 1985. In early 2003, she switched to the flag of North Korea and was renamed **Mohsein** but this was shortlived as she arrived at Alang in India for breaking up on 7 January 2004. She was seen as **Mohsein** on page 29 of *Coasters of the 1950s*.

(John Wiltshire collection)

The **Marwit**, photographed as she made a cautious approach to the entrance to the Manchester Ship canal at Eastham on 7 October 1978, was driven by a 6-cylinder Industrie engine of 600bhp. She was launched at the Slikkerveer yard of De Groot & van Vliet on 26 September 1959 and delivered on 29 December. At first glance she appears to be a conventional coaster but careful observation will spot the tops of tanks in her forward hold. She was built as a chemical carrier and those six tanks carried liquid chlorine from ICI's Castner Kellner works on the Weaver Navigation at Weston Point to Lisahally near Londonderry. In the aft hold was space for 521 pallets used to bring neoprene back to Runcorn on the return voyage. The charter to Dupont for this service began on 6 January 1960 and ended on 1 June 1981, by which time she had completed 1323 round trips. Later in 1981 she was sold to owners in Chittagong and was renamed **Sapna**. Problems soon began and she remained at Chittagong after arriving there from Calcutta on 11 February 1982. On 3 September, her class was suspended with surveys overdue and she was arrested on 29 June 1983. There is no evidence that she ever sailed again. On 14 July 1985 she was reported to have been stranded at Banglabazar and was sold for breaking up which began on 30 March 1986.

(Laurie Schofield)

The later career of this vessel poses some interesting questions. Her early history is easy to trace. She was launched on 4 January 1960 at the Arnhemsche shipyard in Arnhem as **City of Cork** and was delivered to Dublin-based Palgrave Murphy during March. She was powered by an 8-cylinder MAN engine of 1500bhp. Sold to Bugsier in 1971, she was renamed **Levensau**. She left northern Europe for the Mediterranean after purchase in early 1980 by Lebanese owners. She was renamed **Rayes-I** and became **Ahmad 2** five years later. In 1992, she took the names **Hussein 1** and **Tweit VI**, and at some stage during that year was converted to a livestock carrier. Later changes of name saw her become **Pinar Livestock** and then **Al Haj Amin 2** in 1996 and **Al Kawasser II** in 1999. *Lloyd's Register* and all other sources note her next change of name coming in 2004 when she was renamed **Capitaine II**. This photograph suggests something quite different. Taken at Al Hamriyah port in Dubai on 23 August 2002, the ship clearly carries the name **Capitaine III** and she was flying the Lebanese flag. Although one source suggests that the ship is still in service, nothing further is known about her.

(Roger Hurcombe)

The **Pelops** was built by van der Giessen & Zn. Scheepswerven N.V. at Krimpen a/d IJssel for the well-known Dutch company Koninklijke Nederlandsche Stoomboot Maatschappij (KNSM). She was launched on 16 March 1959 and delivered as **Minos** on 16 June. Her 6-cylinder Werkspoor engine of 1800bhp gave her a service speed of 13.25 knots. In December 1972 she was sold to Cypriot owners although management remained with KNSM. This proved to be brief as she was sold on to Greek operators and renamed **Pelops** in 1973. Some sources suggest that she was laid up at Piraeus from 3 July 1985 but this lay up may have begun earlier as this photograph shows her in Piraeus roads on 8 August 1984. She was broken up at Aspropyrgos in Greece during 1985. Some Dutch sources suggest that breaking up began on 25 July but others suggest that it did not begin until September.

(Bernard McCall)

The **Andairon** was very unusual among Dutch coasters of her era, and is almost unique in this book, in being built without masts or cargo handling gear. Launched by Arnhemsche Scheepsbouw in Arnhem on 25 March 1961, this coaster was delivered as **Brittenburgh** to Wm. H. Müller, of Rotterdam, on 23 June. She was driven by an 8-cylinder MAN engine of 1000bhp. During the 1960s, she traded regularly between Rotterdam and the north-east of England, and it was during one of those voyages that she grounded near Redcar on 8 December 1967. She refloated easily and without assistance on the next day. In 1970 she was sold to another Rotterdam company and was renamed **Andairon**, retaining this name when bought by Wealtje Hendrik Roelfs, of Groningen, in mid-1972. During the 1970s, she and the **Biak** (see page 2) ran a weekly liner service to Lisbon from No. 7 Berth in No. 8 Dock, Manchester. In late 1980, she sailed to the Caribbean and passed through the hands of several owners without change of identity until becoming **Junior Jo** in 1992. Her subsequent history is unknown but in 2011 she was noted on her side and semi-submerged in the Suriname River. We see her passing Old Quay Lock at Runcorn when outward bound on the Manchester Ship Canal on 21 September 1975.

(Neil Burns)

The **Erica**, photographed in Piraeus roads on 2 October 1984, was launched at the Waterhuizen shipyard of Gebr. van Diepen on 9 November 1960 and delivered on 18 January of the following year. Named **Aerdenhout**, the original intention had been to name the vessel **Nehim I**. Power came from an 8-cylinder Werkspoor engine of 860bhp. Sold within the Netherlands in early 1970, she was renamed **Spithead**. She left Dutch ownership eight years later when acquired by Galenna Marine Enterprises who renamed her **Galstream**. A partnership had been established between Galenna and Stewart Chartering for the shipping of clay from England to the Mediterranean (see also page 79). Thus she continued to visit ports in northern Europe and was a frequent caller for clay cargoes at ports in south-west England. There followed a series of sales within Greece which saw her become **Erica** (1984), **Portaitissa** (1988), **Billis** (1991), **Dig I** and **Billis** (1995), **Georgia M** (1996), and finally **Sea Sky** (2004). She was sold for breaking up at Aliaga in mid-2006.

(Nigel Jones)

While some coasters had an uneventful career, others had more than their share of problems and the **Plancius** certainly fits in the latter category. She was launched at G. J. van der Werff's Scheepsbouw in Westerbroek on 27 October 1961 and delivered as **Novel** to Arend Brouwer and Frederik Galenkamp, of Kampen, on 27 December. Wagenborg's looked after management even after a sale to Harm Haveman, also of Kampen, in early September 1974. It was at this point that she was renamed **Plancius**. Sold again in 1988 she was renamed **Argo-T** but in December 1990 she was deemed unseaworthy and, despite reports that she had been sold to breakers, she was laid up at Oostmahorn for two years. By June 1993 she was trading once again and was named **Monique**, becoming **Ines I** in 1995,

Martina and then **Vanderpool Express** in July 1996. On 14 July 1997 four people were shot dead on board the ship which was berthed in the Miami River and the ship's engineer was fatally stabbed. The vessel's owners changed her name to **Fidele Express** three days later and in December 1997 were arrested for drug smuggling. On 13 October 1997, the ship grounded on a sandbank when waiting to enter Miami. Renamed **Zion Train** in 2000, she was arrested in June 2001 for non-payment of port dues and was sold to a diving company. On 2 June 2003 she was sunk off Miami as an artificial reef. Astonishingly her troubles were not over as she suffered damage following hurricanes in 2004 and 2005. We see her in the unmistakeable setting of Charlestown on 10 September 1986.

(Cedric Catt)

Once coasters are acquired by Greek operators and given a name that is written in Cyrillic lettering, it is not always easy to trace the history of the vessel. There are added complications when the Greek word Agios, meaning saint, is written as Aghios or simply abbreviated to Ag. We do know enough about the **Agios Dionisios** to be able to follow her career. She was launched at the van Diepen shipyard in Waterhuizen on 1 December 1961 and delivered on 9 February 1962. Named **Prinsenbeek**, she was operated by Spliethoff's, a well-known Amsterdam-based shipping company. Her engine was a 6-cylinder Deutz of 650bhp. She was sold to Cypriot operators in 1971 and renamed **Fulsea** but had to change from

Famagusta registry to Limassol after the unfortunate division of Cyprus in 1974. She then passed through the hands of several Greek owners being renamed **Meropi** (1985), **Georgios Maninis** (1985) and **Saronis** (1990). She hoisted the Bolivian flag as **Aurora** in 1999 but probably never sailed anywhere near South America and she kept the same name when bought by Albanian interests in 2002. She arrived for recycling at Aliaga in mid-January 2008. The **Agios Dionisios** was photographed at Vathi, the main port of the island of Samos, on 25 August 1984.

(Neil Burns)

Ahlmark Lines can trace its origins back to the mid-nineteenth century. Based in the city of Karlstad on Lake Vänern in Sweden, it continues to be an important part of the Scandinavian transport scene. Until the 1950s, many of its new ships had been built in Germany, notably at the Krögerwerft yard in Rendsburg. Attracted by the prices being offered by Dutch yards, it had two coasters built by the De Waal shipyard at Zaltbommel. The first of these was the **Unden**, launched on 28 October 1961 and delivered on 14 December to a Dutch company associated with Ahlmark as it was cheaper to operate the ships under the Dutch flag than Swedish. She was the second Ahlmark ship to carry this name; a Dutch source claims that she was built as **Romulus** with her sister to be **Remus**. She was driven by an 8-cylinder MWM engine of 1050bhp. In 1966 she passed to Finnish owners without change of name but now flying the flag of Finland. We see her as such in the River Ouse on

28 May 1977. She did hoist the Swedish flag in 1985 following purchase by a Stockholm-based company. A sale within Sweden in 1988 saw her renamed **Lunden** but under the flag of St Vincent and the Grenadines. Having arrived at her owner's base in Falkenberg on 21 December 1994, she was soon sold and departed for the Mediterranean being renamed **Stavros Emannuel II**. Later in 1995 she was renamed **Lundeno** and then **Sea Blue** (1998) and **Blacksun** (1999). As such she left Colombia on 7 May 2001 but suspiciously arrived in the Azores named **Helen**. She left as **Saturn** and the authorities were awaiting her when she berthed in Piraeus on 8 September. Hidden in a generator they found 201 kilogrammes of cocaine. The ship was laid up in Perama and eventually arrived at Aliaga for recycling in August 2004.

(David Gallichan)

47

Powered by a 6-cylinder Brons engine of 360bhp, the **Nora** was built at the Waterhuizen shipyard of J. Pattje & Zoon. She was launched on 19 June 1962 and delivered to Wijnne & Barends on 13 September. In April 1974 she came into British ownership and was named **Ekpan Chieftain**, with Penzance as her port of registry. We see her thus named at Par on 3 May 1975. On 29 December 1975 she was arrested at Terneuzen and the owning company was declared bankrupt in February 1976. She was then acquired by Freight Express Seacon, renamed **Ali**, and almost immediately sold on to an owner in Kuwait. A sale within that country saw her renamed **Al Niser 1** in 1978. Her end came two years later when she sank on 23 March 1980. At the time she was on passage from Kuwait to Bombay (Mumbai) with a cargo of copper and iron.

(the late Peter Townsend, Ron Baker collection)

The **Marinus Smits**, named after her owner and managed by Kamp's, differed in appearance from many of the other coasters in this book. She was an open shelterdecker with two goalpost masts, seen clearly in this view of her entering the Bristol Channel from Swansea on 28 May 1971. These masts supported a total of six derricks. She was launched at the De Groot & van Vliet shipyard in Slikkerveer on 14 April 1962 and delivered to Marinus Smits on 13 June. She was driven by a 6-cylinder MAN engine of 1100bhp. Sold within the Netherlands in late October 1973 she was renamed **Susanne Lönborg** but in the following year she was sold to Greek owners and renamed **Christina**. She remained in Greek ownership for the rest of her career but was renamed **Christina II** in 1977, **Elpis** in 1980, and **Notios Hellas** in 1983 and then **Riva** in 1988. As **Notios Hellas** she was laid up and then abandoned at Chioggia. Although in increasingly poor condition, she was not declared a total loss until March 1996 and remained in *Lloyd's Register* until 2002.

(John Wiltshire)

In summer 1959, the Ramsey Steamship Company bought a Dutch coaster on the secondhand market. So pleased were they with this vessel, the 1950-built **Ben Vooar**, that when they began to consider the purchase of a new coaster, they approached Dutch builders in addition to those in the UK. Finding that Dutch yards were also cheaper than British yards, they opted for E. J. Smit & Zoon at Westerbroek, the builders of the **Ben Vooar**. The new vessel, named **Ben Varrey**, was launched on 10 November 1962 but the harsh winter resulted in a delay of six weeks before completion and she was handed over after trials on 14 March 1963. She served her owners well until December 1984 when she had to be towed to Ramsey because of a broken crankshaft. With special survey imminent, the total cost could not be justified. Consequently, she was then laid up and offered for sale. On 1 August 1985 she was sold for breaking up at Millom, arriving there in tow of the tug **Primrose** on 17 September. We see her outward bound in the River Mersey in July 1976.

(David Gallichan)

50

Powered by an 8-cylinder Deutz engine of 620bhp, the *Corrie II* passes beneath the Humber Bridge on 11 July 1983. She was launched at the Groningen yard of J. Vos & Zoon on 29 November 1962 and delivered on 11 June 1963 to Jan Christiaan Hendrik de Vrij although she was initially registered to the builder's own account. In mid-July 1986 ownership was taken over by J. Rotman & Sons, based in Groningen, and the coaster was renamed *Rola*. Sold on in March 1990, she was renamed *Miska* but she was laid up at Den Helder in October 1999 because of the financial problems of her owners. On 29 August 2000, she was sold at auction at the request of the Rabo Hypotheekbank, of Amsterdam. The buyers planned to convert her to a party ship but a month later she was sold on and converted to a barge named *Nijverheid* for trade on inland waterways. She was soon employed in the sand trade between Harlingen and Drachten. Sold again in 2007, she was then converted to a passenger vessel and, named *Andere Boeg*, has continued in this role with accommodation for 90 people.

(David Gallichan)

The photographer was remarkably fortunate to obtain a photograph of this vessel when she was named *Otter*. She is one of the most frequently renamed vessels in this book and bore the name *Otter* only between May 1984 and July 1985 and is seen at Par on 21 September 1984. She began life at the 'De Hoop' shipyard at Lobith-Tolkamer on the northern bank of the River Rhein between Nijmegen and Duisburg. The southern bank at this point is German territory. The ship was launched on 16 March 1963 and was delivered as *Valkenier* on 15 May. Her engine was a 6-cylinder Industrie of 693bhp. After only three years in service she was sold to owners in Dunkirk and was renamed *Topaze* under the French flag. When lying off Algiers on the night of 11/12 December 1967, she ran aground after her anchor cable parted. She was not refloated until September 1968 when she

was sold to a local shipyard. In 1969 she was bought by a Somali shipping company and was renamed *Bababraham* but after making a single voyage reverted to French ownership as *Kernoa*. Remarkably she returned to Dutch ownership in mid-August 1973 and now became *Lizard*. Further sales within the Netherlands saw her become *Demark* (1976), *Amie* (1980) and *Vlotter* (1983). Soon after acquiring this name in March 1983, she suffered serious bow damage after colliding with the Russian *Baltiyskiy 66* off the Hook of Holland on 22 April 1983. The buyers in May 1984 were Maltese-flag operators who gave her the name *Otter*. Her final name was *Reef Moon*, given to her by operators who traded her out of Mombasa under the flag of St Vincent & the Grenadines. On 12 April 1988 she arrived at Gadani Beach for breaking up.

(Cedric Catt)

After thick ice had been removed from the fairway, this vessel was launched as **Breewijd** for P. A. van Es & Co. at D. & J. Boot's 'De Vooruitgang' shipyard in Alphen aan den Rijn on 7 February 1963. She was delivered, though, as **Kittiwake** on 23 May, An open shelterdecker, she was powered by a 6-cylinder Industrie engine of 1350bhp. She was acquired by Danish owner Ebbe Folkmar in 1973 who had just left his job as head of the shipping department at van Es and was given permission to buy the **Kittiwake**. Renamed **Svendborg Grace** the ship proved expensive to operate in the 1970s. After spending most of 1985 in Søby she was sold and renamed **Anne M**. Under this name she arrived at Famagusta in Cyprus on 11 August 1993 and was detained there after weapons and explosives were allegedly found on board. The owner was not prepared to pay off the authorities in Famagusta and the ship became the subject of diplomatic discussions at government level. In 1996 the **Anne M** was confiscated and sold to Turkish operators and renamed **Kaptan Resat Akbas**. She was photographed as such in Istanbul roads on 21 June 2003. Her final three years in service were marked by three groundings. The first of these was comparatively minor. On 17 October 2005, she ran aground briefly while on passage from Izmir to Haifa. Then on 27 April 2008, she grounded on the Greek coast at the start of a voyage to Tuzla and on 11 October 2008, again heading for Tuzla from Greece, she grounded this time on the Turkish coast. By the end of the year, she had arrived at Aliaga for recycling.

(Nigel Jones)

The ***Twee Gezusters*** had just left Goole when photographed on 23 February 1979. She was launched at the Westerbroek yard of E. J. Smit & Zoon on 5 April 1963 and delivered on 18 June to brothers Jan Damhof Sr. and Harm Damhof, of Delfzijl. She was driven by a 16-cylinder Brons engine of 1250bhp. In October 1967, the vessel was acquired by Henderika Damhof-Schrik, widow of Harm, and Jan Damhof, Harm's son. Often used for bringing fruit from the Mediterranean to north-west Europe, the ship was involved in a tragic incident when she caught fire on 19 May 1973 not long after leaving Algiers and heading for Sète with a cargo that included cork and containers. The fire started in the cork and the crew flooded the hold as the ship was being towed back to Algiers. The 30 degree list was resolved once the water had been pumped out. Over the following week, the damaged cargo was removed and it was then that the charred bodies of six stowaways were discovered. No doubt they had been responsible for starting the fire. The ship was laid up for sale in 1984 and was sold to Caribbean operators in July of that year. She was transferred to the flag of Panama and renamed ***Two Sisters***, the English meaning of her original Dutch name. She remained under the Panamanian flag when sold and renamed ***Nabajot*** in February 1993. In July 1998 she grounded at Balboa and was abandoned. Later reports claim that she was broken up in situ.

(David Gallichan)

The **Victress**, seen outward bound in the River Ouse at Goole in April 1976, was built at the Bodewes yard in Martenshoek. She was launched on 20 December 1962 and delivered to Beck's Scheepvaartkantoor on 23 April 1963. Her engine was a 6-cylinder Brons of 360bhp. The **Victress** remained in Beck ownership until June 1981 when she was acquired by British owners and renamed **Thamwell**, the name being a combination of Thames and Orwell.

The **Thamwell** was photographed passing Meredyke inward bound in the River Trent on 24 June 1983. The next sale saw her move to Cornish ownership and she was suitably renamed **Maenporth**, retaining this name after transferring to the Honduran flag in 1990. On 25 August 1991, she suffered engine damage when off the Isle of Wight and had to be towed to Portsmouth. Following repairs, she resumed her voyage on 12 September. After arriving in Rotterdam from Charlestown on 17 May 1992, she was laid up awaiting sale. Sold in late summer and renamed **Marystan**, she left Rotterdam on 3 October and sailed via Europoort, Antwerp, Plymouth and Las Palmas to Demerara. She then began a regular service linking Demerara to Port of Spain. In late December 1995 she was reported to have been laid up at Demerara and remained there a decade later. Nothing further is known.

(both David Gallichan)

We should not forget that Dutch shipyards were also building some fine tankers. With the original name of this tanker still evident on the ship's hull, there is no doubt that she is the same vessel as that in the photograph below. However when she was photographed at Al Hamriyah port in Dubai on 21 October 1999, she was named *Qais-1* and there is no other evidence that she ever bore this name. She was deleted from *Lloyd's Register* in 2002.

(Roger Hurcombe)

Launched at the Slikkerveer yard of De Groot and van Vliet on 14 December 1963, this tanker was delivered to Tankvaart Rotterdam on 15 April 1964 as **Dutch Engineer**. In 1973, the well-known Dutch tanker operator Gebr. Broere took over management. This company had been founded in November 1923 by the brothers Jacobus and Bastiaan Broere and the black funnels with white letters GB on a blue band became a common sight on coastal tankers throughout northern Europe. In 1978 the **Dutch Engineer** was sold to British owners. She retained her original name until 1981 when she became **Tees Redwing**. Sold to Greek owners in 1987, she was renamed **Vasilios XII** and then became **Gulf Maid** under the Panamanian flag ten years later. In May 1988 Gebr. Broere became part of the Royal Pakhoed Group and subsequent takeovers and mergers saw the remaining tankers eventually join the Essberger fleet.

(David Gallichan)

In the mid-1960s, three stylish tankers were built for Gebr. de Haas by Nieuwe Noord-Nederlandsche Scheepswerven in Groningen. The third of these was launched on 3 April 1965 and delivered to de Haas as **Mare Silentum** on 16 June. She was photographed at Avonmouth on 21 April 1968 with **Esso Glasgow** in the background. In October 1970, she was lengthened by 12,2 metres and deepened at Vlaardingen. Two years later, Nederlandsche Scheepvaart Unie (later to become Nedlloyd) acquired a 50% interest in the de Haas company and took the remaining 50% in October 1973. The name of the owning company was changed to Nedlloyd Bulkchem in mid-September 1977 but the vessels in the fleet retained their original names. It was in late summer 1985 that the **Mare Silentum** left northern Europe for the Mediterranean. She was bought by Greek owners and renamed **Vasilios IX**. A sale within Greece saw her become **Samos** in September 2004. Seven years later she was sold for breaking up and arrived at Aliaga on 13 September 2011.

(John Wiltshire)

We return briefly to 1964 for this photograph. Powered by a 5-cylinder Brons engine of 300bhp, the **Twebro** was built by Scheepswerf 'Appingedam' v/h A. Apol at Appingedam and was launched on 9 April 1964. She was delivered to brothers Albert and Hendrik Huisman, of Zwartsluis, on 12 June. In 1977 she had the misfortune to spend 41 days trapped in the River Hull. Having passed under the raised Drypool Bridge over the river, the bridge jammed and it was over a month before the bridge could be lifted to release the ship. Management of the **Twebro** was in the hands of Wijnne & Barends until 1979 when she was sold without change of name to an owner in Arkel. Her first and only change of identity came in 1987 when she was acquired by Honduran-flag operators by whom she was renamed **Residu**. Her end came on 18 June 1992 when she was on passage from Northwich to Drogheda with a cargo of sodium carbonate. She began to leak and listed to 20° when about 20 miles off Llandudno. Her crew hoped to take her to the Isle of Man but conditions worsened and they were taken off by helicopter. She eventually sank a few hours later. We see her as **Twebro** leaving Aberdeen on a sunny afternoon in April 1979.

(Alastair Paterson)

Launched at the Appingedam v/h A. Apol shipyard on 25 March 1965, the **Fastnet** was delivered to Jan Klugkist on 22 June. She was driven by an 8-cylinder Brons engine of 600bhp. Although registered in the Netherlands, the coaster was managed by the owner's Neptune Shipping Company, based in Dublin, and saw service on the Atlantic Steam Navigation Company's container service linking Preston to several ports on the east coast of Ireland. The late 1980s saw ownership change on several occasions but she retained the name **Fastnet**. After problems in the Humber estuary in late October 1991, she arrived in Hull on 24 October and remained there until departing to Zeebrugge for lay up on 12 September 1992. The story then becomes quite obscure. Sold in 1993, she was renamed **Carat** but

seems never to have sailed under this name. Later in the year, she became **Tina I** and as such left Zeebrugge for Antwerp on 29 October 1993. She left Antwerp for Rupelmonde on 14 December and returned ten days later. Her next reported movement saw her leaving Antwerp for Apapa/Lagos as **Tina I** on 14 January 1994. There is a report that she was renamed **Monica I** on 30 June 1994 and then **Monica II** on 18 July. Although understood to have been renamed **Nico** in June 1998, the remainder of her career is unclear but she is reported to have arrived at Hoylandsbygd in Norway for breaking up in mid-July 2002. We see her in the River Parrett on 19 July 1989 as she heads for Dunball Wharf with a cargo of fertiliser from Saint Malo.

(Bernard McCall collection)

Awaiting a call to a berth at Fowey to load china clay on 6 May 1973 is the **Herman Bodewes**. Driven by an 8-cylinder Deutz engine of 1060bhp, she was launched at the Bodewes shipyard in Martenshoek on 7 April 1965 and delivered on 2 June to Herman Bodewes Martenshoek, the letters HBM being just visible on this image. In fact, a 1/3000 share was owned by Gerardus Wijnandus Bodewes and the remaining 2999 shares were owned by N.V. Maatschappij tot Exploitatie van Scheepswerven. She was sold in January 1977 and was renamed **Rena Z** under the Panamanian flag. Later changes of identity saw her become **Ataner** (1984), **Manjee Star** (1985) and finally **Express Star** (1986). She arrived at Gadani Beach on 1 September 1987 and was beached for recycling three days later.

(Terry Nelder)

The **Breewijd**, photographed at Par on 19 July 1971, was built at the Alphen aan den Rijn shipyard of 'De Vooruitgang' v/h D. Boot for well-known Rotterdam-based owner P. A. van Es & Co. Driven by an 8-cylinder Industrie engine of 1000bhp, she was launched on 12 November 1964 and delivered on 22 January 1965. After nine years in the van Es fleet, she was acquired by International Shipbrokers and renamed **Albert V**, replacing the coaster of that name seen on page 16. A decade later she was sold to owners in Piraeus and was renamed **Ikaros**. After a further ten years she was sold to Syrian owners and renamed **Shams Ddin 3**. There is some confusion about the date of her conversion to a livestock carrier. This conversion took place in August 1994 and not 2001 as noted by one Dutch source and certainly not 1965 as noted by *Lloyd's Register*. Her last reported movement was at Kuwait in 1998 but her name is understood to have been modified to **Shamsddin III** in 2001 and one source suggests that she was seen at Yemen in 2008. Once again her ultimate fate is unknown. We do not often publish views taken from the quayside but there are exceptions and this is one because this image clearly shows her unusual funnel design.

(the late Peter Townsend, Ron Baker collection)

The **Comtesse** was launched at the Martenshoek shipyard of Bodewes Scheepswerven on 15 April 1965 and delivered to Beck's Scheepvaartkantoor on 30 June. Power came from a 12-cylinder Brons engine of 900bhp. We see her in the River Ouse on 9 December 1978. After twenty years in the Beck fleet she was sold to Greek owners and was renamed **Nikolis Pallis**. She continued to visit northern Europe, often loading cargoes of clay at ports in south-west England. From that time on, however, she was dogged by problems. She was detained in port on several occasions and she also managed to run aground. On 15 September 1989, she grounded on rocks near Mandhili Island in Greece. Then on 19 May 1995 while carrying out engine trials she grounded on soft mud by a fish farm near

Salamis, refloating a week later after some cargo had been removed. She was arrested by salvors pending security but she disappeared on 22 December. She was found in Vassiliko Bay, Cyprus, using a false name on 24 January 1996. On 28 February she arrived at Larnaca in tow and was arrested. She was towed to Limassol on 3 May and from there to Lattakia on 21 June. At some stage in all this she was sold and renamed **Maria**. By 1997 she was sold to Syrian owners and renamed **Bahlawan**, becoming **Basha I** in 2006. Needless to say, incidents continued and, astonishingly, she is reported to be still in service in mid-2014.

(David Gallichan)

One would imagine that a vessel named **Paraguay Speed** would be trading either within South America or to/from that area and that certainly applied in this instance. The photograph was taken as she left the River Trent bound for Hamburg on 23 March 1982. She left Hamburg six days later heading for Asunción in Paraguay. The coaster was built by Scheepswerf- en Reparatiebedrijf Harlingen. She was launched as **Solent** on 3 September 1965 and delivered to her owners after successful trials on the Waddenzee on 10 November. Power came from a 6-cylinder MAK engine of 750bhp. In early 1968 she returned to trade after being lengthened by 4,5 metres. In mid-November 1975 she was bought by a Hamburg-based owner who transferred her to the Cypriot flag and renamed her **Bodensee**. She remained under that flag when renamed **Paraguay Speed** in 1982. A further renaming saw her become **Pearl** in 1985. On 3 January 1987 she arrived at the German port of Husum for breaking up which began in May of that year.

(David Gallichan)

It was in 1952 that Otto Danielsen, based in Copenhagen, became a ship owner. He would go on to have close links with the Netherlands and had many ships built there. One of these was the **Ulla Danielsen**, launched at the Westerbroek yard of E. J. Smit & Zoon on 15 December 1965 and delivered on 11 March 1966. She was the third vessel in the fleet to be named after the founder's granddaughter. The ship was driven by a 6-cylinder MAK engine of 800bhp. After only five years in the Danielsen fleet she was sold to Dutch owners and renamed **Ulla** with management by Oost Atlantic Lijn, of Rotterdam. Two years later she was sold and renamed **Cornelia B VI** and then in 1978 she came into the ownership of Oost Atlantic Lijn and was renamed **Atlantic Breeze**, thus following this company's tradition of naming ships **Atlantic _____**. She is seen in the River Mersey at Eastham on 11 August 1979. Sold within the Netherlands in 1981, she was renamed **Anna** and kept this name after purchase by a South African company in 1983. For the next eight years she traded between Durban and ports in Mozambique. After lying in Durban between mid-March and June 1991, she was acquired by Syrian owners and renamed **Lina S**. She became **Al Asaad I** in 1994 and then **Gaafar S** in 2001. This must have been brief as she was reported to have been broken up in that year.

(Laurie Schofield)

In the mid-1960s, the Blue Star Line bought four coasters in order to tranship cargo to and from its ocean-going vessels. The first two were second-hand purchases but then it bought two new vessels, the first of which was the **Deben**. Launched at the Boele's shipyard in Bolnes on 18 February 1966, she was delivered in the following month. Her engine was a 6-cylinder Blackstone of 530bhp. In 1971 she was sold to Mardorf, Peach & Co Ltd and was renamed **Gretchen Weston**. A further five years elapsed and in January 1976 she entered the fleet of the Ramsey Steamship Co Ltd as **Ben Ain**. On 3 November 1981 she suffered engine failure whilst on passage from Peel to Garston and was towed to Ramsey for repairs. She arrived at Douglas from Glasson Dock on 12 April 1991 and left on 9 June following sale to a Cypriot-flag owner by whom she was renamed **Prince**. After calling at Flushing, Amsterdam and New Holland, she headed for the Mediterranean via El Ferrol and Ceuta. She was to experience problems, though. August saw her towed from Rhodes to Limassol and then to Tripoli (Lebanon) and in October she was towed back from Tripoli to Limassol. Seven years later she became **Abdoulah** and then **Abdoulah I** for Lebanese owners although flying the flag of Bolivia. On 8 September 2001, she grounded off the coast of Oman when on passage from Dubai to Somalia. The wreck was later dismantled.

(John Wiltshire)

The **Sambre** makes a cautious approach to the lock at Barry on the evening of 17 April 1976. Like many other examples, by this time she retained her masts but her derricks had been removed. Built by Scheepswerf 'Appingedam' v/h A. Apol at Appingedam, she was launched on 9 September 1965 and on 5 November was delivered to a Groningen-based consortium with Kamp's as managers. Power came from a 5-cylinder Kromhout engine of 336bhp. A low air draught vessel, she was designed by Goedkoop N.V. in Delfzijl for trading up the River Seine to Paris. In 1981 she was sold to Caribbean operators and left Flushing on 13 July, heading initially for Las Palmas. She was at Kingston (Jamaica) by mid-August. Renamed **Jeleta** the following year, she became **Miss BJ** in 1985 and, as such, was sunk in the Bahamas as an artificial reef on 22 June 1999.

(Nigel Jones)

In the latter half of the 1950s, Carebeka decided to own ships on its own account. This decision ultimately led to the collapse of the company because building and owning ships was a very different business from managing them on behalf of captain/owners. The first owned ship was completed in February 1957. Despite disappointing trading results, new ships were to be built for the fleet and the **Carebeka IV** was ordered in 1964. Launched on 30 December 1965 at the J. Pattje yard in Waterhuizen, she was delivered to Carebeka on 29 April 1966. She had an 8-cylinder Industrie engine of 745bhp. During spring 1970, she was lengthened by 7,57 metres at the Niestern shipyard in Groningen. On 11 May 1973 she collided with the Norwegian ore carrier **Bjorghav** in the Straits of Dover and the extensive

damage took a month to repair. We see her outward bound from Plymouth on 5 September 1973. In 1977 she was sold to Cypriot-flag operators and was renamed **Skymina**. Four years later, she became **Alexfay** under the Greek flag and then **Maro** in 1987. A switch to the flag of St Vincent & the Grenadines in 1988 accompanied the change of name to **Senior** and then she became **Hassan** for Syrian owners in the following year. On 20 January 1999 she grounded on rocks off Tripoli and was refloated ten days later. She then seems to have been laid up at Lattakia until sold to breakers at Aliaga where she arrived on 25 September 2001.

(the late Peter Townsend, World Ship Photo Library)

A half shelterdeck vessel, the **Gerda Smits** loads china clay at Fowey on 25 July 1975. She was launched on 17 September 1966 at the de Groot & van Vliet yard in Slikkerveer and on 1 November was delivered as **Nordstrand Priva** to owners based in the Danish port of Sønderborg. Remaining within Denmark, she became **Nordstrand Partner** in 1968 but was acquired by Marinus Smits, of Rotterdam, and renamed **Gerda Smits** in April 1969. As with other Smits vessels, management was entrusted to Kamp's but was transferred to GenChart in 1976. In 1973 she was returned to her building yard to be lengthened by eight metres. Sold within the Netherlands in late 1981, she was renamed **Anna Heida**. She left Rotterdam as **Lady Dalal** on 27 March 1989 with Beirut as her destination after being sold to operators based in Lebanon. In late November 2001 she transferred to the flag of Tonga and was renamed **Ranim J**, becoming **Mamoun B** in 2002, and **Piero** then, under the North Korean flag, **Proton** in 2003. She arrived at Piraeus from Alexandria on 25 October 2003 and was laid up at the Greek port. Eventually sold at auction on 7 November 2007, she was renamed **Prot** and switched to the flag of Comoros. She left Piraeus on 22 November, supposedly heading for Turkey "to commence repairs" but in fact she was beached at Aliaga for breaking up just six days later.

(the late Peter Townsend, Ron Baker collection)

After taking over as master of another vessel, Captain Bernhard Borghorst, of Haren-Ems in Germany, decided to have his own coaster and this was the **Margareta-B** which Captain Borghorst ordered from the Westerbroek shipyard. Completed in July 1966, she was driven by a 6-cylinder MWM engine of 300bhp. She was put under the management of Wagenborg. Her maiden voyage saw her carrying salt from Hengelo to France and she then worked on a liner service between France, England and the Netherlands. On 27 December 1973, she was bought by Cork-based Marine Transport Services, and renamed **Marloag**. She was thus named when photographed leaving Par on 10 May 1976. Four years later she came under the Red Ensign as **Eskspring**, becoming **Minories** in 1979. The next name change was easily effected as she became **Minor** in 1981 and finally **Jane** in 1983. It was not until early 2012 that she was deleted from registers, her continued existence by then in doubt.

(the late Peter Townsend, Ron Baker collection)

This coaster replaced another of the same name that had been built only two years previously but had sunk off the Belgian coast after hitting a submerged wreck. The **Neutron** seen above was built at the Bodewes Gruno shipyard in Foxhol where she was launched in June 1966 and delivered at the end of the following month to Beck's Scheepvaartkantoor N.V. in Groningen. She had a 6-cylinder Brons engine of 375bhp. She was evidently quite new when photographed at Ipswich on 13 August 1966. In mid-March 1981, she came under the British flag as **Hydrus** and retained this name after switching to the Maltese flag in 1985. Sold and renamed **Renee** in 1987, she arrived in Rotterdam from Great Yarmouth on 23 February 1990 and was reported as sold during the summer. She departed from Rotterdam on 11 August and sailed via IJmuiden to St Michael's (Ponta Delgada) and eventually arrived at Port of Spain on 16 October. Published sources make no reference to this sale, the next one being reported to operators based in Anguilla in 1992. Nothing further is known and she was deleted from registers in 2012, her continued existence being in doubt.

(John Wiltshire)

This vessel can claim to have one of the more interesting histories in this book. Launched at the Gebr. Coops shipyard in Hoogezand on 8 June 1966, she was delivered as **Lumey** to Gerrit Dost, of Groningen, on 7 July. Management was in the hands of Wijnne & Barends who continued as managers after the coaster was sold to a Groningen-based partnership and renamed **Esperance** in January 1975. This management ceased in May 1977 when another sale saw the ship remain in Dutch ownership but now named **Espero** and flying the flag of Panama. The same owners renamed her **Vios** in 1978 and then brought her back to the Dutch flag in 1983. She was still flying the flag of Panama when photographed in the River Ouse on 4 September 1979. On 28 September 1984, she was sold again - twice on the same day. Bought by the Ferus Smit shipyard, she was resold on that day to a

Delfzijl-based partnership, becoming **Nescio** and entering Wagenborg management. A further sale in 1988 saw her renamed **Alcion**. In June 1990 her class was withdrawn and in mid-October she was sold for use as a repair ship. The next four years saw a series of sales and the removal of her main engine. In 1995, however, she was fitted with a new Cummins main engine of 500bhp and was rebuilt as a passenger vessel for 200 people. Now renamed **Thalassa Royal** she was totally unrecognisable as a former coaster. She became **Grace Kelly** after a further sale in 2011. When built she had a 6-cylinder Stork engine of 380bhp. This was replaced by another 6-cylinder Stork engine of 386bhp in February 1980.

(Laurie Schofield)

We have a panoramic view of the **Watum** as she is about to pass beneath the Severn Bridge outward bound from Sharpness on 22 June 1979. Driven by a 6-cylinder MWM engine of 950bhp, the **Watum** is one of the more powerful vessels to feature in this book. She was built by the Nieuwe Noord-Nederlandsche Scheepswerven at Groningen, being launched on 2 June 1966 and delivered to Jannes Reint Bonninga, of Groningen, as **Agua** on 14 July. In June 1974 she entered the Damhof fleet, based in Delfzijl, and was renamed **Watum**. After trading for Damhof for five years, she was sold to owners in India and was renamed **Nicotrade** under the Indian flag. She was noted at Madras on 18 February 1980. She is thought to be still in existence although there have been no recent reports of movements.

(Cedric Catt)

An open shelterdecker, this vessel was launched at the Westerbroek yard of J. Pattje & Zoon on 12 January 1967 and delivered as **Aukes** to owners in Amsterdam on 7 April. Management was entrusted to Spliethoff's, also of Amsterdam, and this company became more involved in ownership in 1969 when the ship was renamed **Raamgracht**, a more typical Spliethoff name. At this time she was converted to a closed shelterdecker at the Welgelegen shipyard in Harlingen. In mid-June 1973 she was bought by Jan Damhof Sr., of Delfzijl, and renamed **Wendy**. She was laid up after arrival at Delfzijl in early April 1986 and some six months later was sold to Caribbean operators although registered in Valletta. She left Antwerp for Las Palmas and Port au Prince on 22 October 1986. She retained the name **Wendy** until she sank off Roatán Island, Honduras, on 21 December 1989. The raised letters of her previous name were still visible when this photograph was taken of her in the River Ouse on 28 April 1980.

(David Gallichan)

This coaster was launched at the Bodewes shipyard in Hoogezand on 10 April 1967 and delivered to Dampskibsselskabet Solnæs as *Grimaldi* on 28 June. Her engine was a 6-cylinder MaK of 750bhp. On 22 August 1969, she collided with the Italian tanker *Ircania* in the Straits of Gibraltar while on passage from Cagliari to Kemitra in ballast. Sold within Denmark in November 1973, she was renamed *Brigit* by owners Finn J Poulsen and Captain Steen Rasmussen. Two years later, she was bought by Marpro Ltd and transferred to the flag of Singapore as *Mariyos City*. On 7 February 1980, she collided with the tanker *Lake Anja* in the Western Approaches soon after starting a voyage from Teignmouth to Barcelona with china clay. Her stem was holed and forepeak flooded. She was escorted back to Devon and her cargo was discharged at Teignmouth. She then sailed to Goole for permanent repairs, arriving on 24 February. In early 1981 she was sold to buyers in Malaysia and was renamed *Hamidah*. Whilst heading to Port Klang on 9 February 1982, she suffered engine problems and diverted to Singapore for repairs. With continued existence in doubt, she was deleted from registers in February 2012. She was photographed in Singapore Roads on 17 June 1999.

(Nigel Jones)

The **Manadotua** was launched at the van Diepen shipyard in Waterhuizen on 22 December 1966 and delivered to a company in Rotterdam as **Valkenswaard** on 13 February 1967. An open shelterdecker, she was driven by an 8-cylinder Werkspoor engine of 940bhp. Sold to Jan Damhof Jr. in November 1975, she was renamed **Geziena** and switched from Rotterdam to Delfzijl registry. Two years later, she left Europe after being purchased by owners in Indonesia. She was renamed **Niaga XVII** and was registered in Surabaya. A sale within Indonesia saw her become **Manadotua** in 1989. She was thought to remain in service in 2014 although removed from the Indonesian register in 2007. She was photographed at anchor off Jakarta on 24 July 2002.

(Nigel Jones)

Launched by Zaanlandsche Scheepsbouw on 11 March 1967, this vessel was delivered as **Annemarie Böhmer** to owners in Rotterdam on 12 May. A closed shelterdecker, she was driven by a 6-cylinder Werkspoor engine of 1550bhp which gave her a service speed of 13 knots. She was sold to the Libyan government in May 1972 and was renamed **Sabratha**. She is seen southbound in the Suez Canal on 21 June 1994. On 19 November 1997, she suffered major engine problems when off the coast of Sardinia and she was towed to Augusta. There it was ascertained that a new crankshaft was needed but no spare parts could be obtained and on 14 May 1998 the ship left Augusta in tow for Homs in Libya where she was to be scrapped. That clearly never happened and eight years later she was bought by a Syrian owner, renamed **Seomar** and registered in Sierra Leone. She became **Diena Green** in 2008 and **Mona Lissa** in 2012. She was thus named when she passed through the Panama Canal in September 2014.

(Nigel Jones)

The vessels on this page and the next are sisterships from a series of ten vessels delivered from four different Dutch shipyards. The order was mediated by Otto Danielsen who was the general agent for Nescos, a sales organisation acting for several yards. The *Toroneos II* was built at the Westerbroek shipyard of E. J. Smit & Zoon and delivered to Danish owner Knud I Larsen as *Nikolaj Sif* on 6 April 1967. Power came from a 6-cylinder Atlas-MaK engine of 1000bhp. Her single hold had two hatches served by three 3-tonne derricks. Sold in 1979, she was renamed *Tender Ship* and then in 1982 she was renamed *Boringia* under the flag of Gibraltar. She arrived at Barry as such on 17 February 1984 and lay up awaiting sale. Visible in the middle distance is the Dock Office at Barry that had recently suffered a serious fire. Sold and renamed *Toroneos II* in mid-June, she departed for Par on 28 June, loading clay for her delivery voyage to the Mediterranean. She passed through the hands of various owners during the later 1980s and 1990s, becoming *Angelika 2* (1985), *Olympic Sun* and then *Olympic Med* in 1988, *Manda Glory* (1995), *Panther* and then *Sweet Spirit* (1996). For most of this time she was trading between Alexandria and Greek ports. Her later names were *San Nicolas* (2000), *Defiant* (2001), and finally *Assos I* (2005). She does not appear under these names in movement reports. She arrived at Aliaga for breaking up in late July 2010.

(Bernard McCall)

The *Agiantonis*, photographed at Piraeus on 18 June 2007, was built at the Bodewes shipyard in Hoogezand. Her engine, like that of the *Toroneos II*, was also a 6-cylinder MaK of 1001bhp. She was delivered as *Leon Sif* to Knud I Larsen in June 1967. In 1979 she became *Tramp Ship 1* under the Panamanian flag and three years later was renamed *Hafnia* for trade under the flag of Gibraltar. It was in 1986 that she became *Agiantonis* when bought by Greek owners. She retained this name until sold in July 2014 for recycling at Aliaga. On 9 August 2001, she suffered a fire in her accommodation area when berthed at the Greek port of Volos. Sadly one crewman was killed.

(Nigel Jones)

The **Trader Ship**, approaching the lock at Sharpness on 14 May 1980, was launched by Scheepswerf Hoogezand N.V. Jac Bodewes at Bergum on 26 May 1967 and delivered to Knud I Larsen as **Holger Sif** on 2 September. Her engine was virtually identical to that of her sisterships. She was to prove less fortunate than her sisters. Renamed **Falstria** in 1982, she arrived at Sharpness on 22 February 1983 and had a fire in her accommodation area. She was then laid up and eventually sold and renamed **Gun**. She left Sharpness on 8 May 1985. She became **Alex G** and then **Four Sea** in 1987, **Irene** and then **Saint James** in 1989. Under the latter name, she left Safi for Ravenna on 20 January 1990 and subsequently ran aground. Towed to Trapani, she arrived on 30 January and remained until 4 December when she sailed to Venice and then on to Piraeus, arriving on 27 December. She remained laid up throughout 1991 and was eventually sold and renamed **Jerez** in Spring 1992, leaving Piraeus on 11 May and resuming her previous trading pattern in the western Mediterranean. In 1996, she was bought by Syrian interests and renamed **Atiat Allah**. After becoming **Emirates 2** in 2003, her final name was **Teeba** in 2007. As such she arrived at Gadani Beach for breaking up in mid-December 2011.

(Cedric Catt)

In addition to building ships for ownership in the Netherlands, Dutch yards built for owners in other countries too and the finished vessels often looked very different from those destined for compatriots. A good example of this was the **Hyde Park**, built by E. J. Smit at Westerbroek for Park Steamships Ltd, London. In fact, the origins of this vessel lie with Danish shipowner Otto Danielsen whose Danish-flagged coasters had found it difficult to trade profitably in the 1960s. Danielsen bought a majority shareholding in Park Steamships Ltd and ordered two vessels, the **Hyde Park** being the second. She was launched on 17 October 1968 and delivered on 12 December. She did come into Danish ownership in December 1972

when she was renamed **Philip Lønborg**. Two years later Icelandic buyers renamed her **Isborg** and then **Sudri** in 1976. In the following year she left northern Europe for the Mediterranean when bought by Greek owners and renamed **Phoenicia**. The next sale saw her become **La Palma** for Lebanese owners in 1982 and she was converted to a livestock carrier in 1991. Further changes of identity saw her become **Berger A** in 1992, **Rihab** in 2003 and **Beccaria** in 2013. She continues to trade in late 2014. We see her as **Berger A** in the Suez Canal on 26 May 1996.

(Nigel Jones)

By the time that we reach the late 1960s, naval architects were designing ships of much greater capacity than had been the case two decades previously and as we have been discovering these were attractive to secondhand buyers throughout the world. The **Seven Seas** was launched at the Harlingen yard of N.V. Scheepswerf-en Reparatiebedrijf 'Harlingen' on 29 November 1968 and delivered on 28 February 1969 to a consortium of five local owners in two families. Power came from an 8-cylinder Industrie engine of 1500bhp. On 30 July 1985 she arrived at Harlingen from Rotterdam and was laid up for sale. Almost a year later she was sold and renamed **World Peace** under the flag of Gibraltar. In the early 1990s, she was a common sight in ports in south-west England as on 21 February 1991 she had been acquired by Galenna Marine Enterprises, a Greek company and renamed **Galseas** (see page 44). Sold within Greece on 6 December 1995, she was renamed **Agios Andreas**. The next eight years saw her renamed on eight occasions and she was involved in various incidents. The last one of these occurred on 20 December 2006 when she grounded on Esek island at the entrance to the Bosphorus. She was subsequently refloated and towed to Aliaga for recycling.

(David Gallichan)

For our final image, we go back a year to 1968. Of 499grt and with two masts and two derricks when built, this vessel is often considered to be the last true "classic" Dutch coaster to have been constructed. Built at Hoogezand by N.V. Scheepswerf 'Voorwaarts' v/h. E. J. Hijlkema, she was launched as **Constance** on 28 February 1968 and delivered on 24 April to Wijnne & Barends. She was the third of her type, following the **Clarissa** and **Claudia** for the same owner. Of special note was her ability to accommodate in her hold long and awkwardly shaped pieces of equipment. Power came from a 6-cylinder Brons engine of 560bhp. In late September 1977 she was sold to Vale Shipping, of Dublin, with Arklow Shipping as managers and she was renamed **Arklow Bridge** under the Irish flag but she kept the familiar scarlet/orange hull of her previous Dutch owner. In 1991, she was acquired by Carisbrooke Shipping and renamed **Mark C** whilst retaining her Dublin registry. Indeed this continued when she was bought by Harris & Dixon (Shipbrokers) Ltd and renamed **Courtfield** in 1985. In 1991, she was bought by Caribbean operators and left Shoreham on 25 July 1991, being next reported at Mobile on 14 September and then Puerto Cabello two weeks later. She subsequently became **Briana** (1995), **Solution** and the **Sea Boekanier** (both in 1996). On 8 March 1997, she heeled over and sank when eighteen miles north of Nuevitas (Cuba). Her crew was rescued. She was photographed in the River Mersey at Eastham on 15 August 1979.

(David Gallichan)